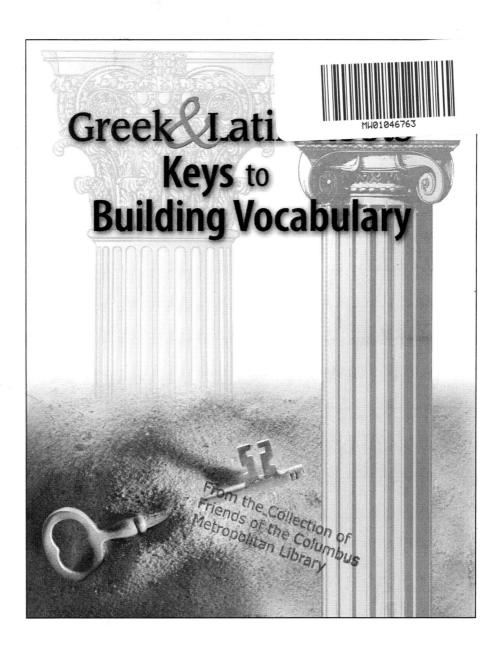

Greek&Latin Roots
Keys to
Building Vocabulary

Authors
Timothy Rasinski, Ph.D., Nancy Padak, Ed.D.,
Rick M. Newton, Ph.D., and Evangeline Newton, Ph.D.
Foreword by Karen Bromley, Ph.D.

SHELL EDUCATION

Greek and Latin Roots: Keys to Building Vocabulary

Editor
Blane Conklin, Ph.D.

Assistant Editor
Leslie Huber, M.A.

Editorial Director
Lori Kamola, M.S.Ed.

Editor-in-Chief
Sharon Coan, M.S.Ed.

Editorial Manager
Gisela Lee, M.A.

Consultant
Joan Irwin, M.A.

Creative Director
Lee Aucoin

Print Production Manager
Don Tran

Interior Layout Designer
Robin Erickson

Print Production
Juan Chavolla

Publisher
Corinne Burton, M.A.Ed.

5301 Oceanus Drive
Huntington Beach, CA 92649-1030
http://www.shelleducation.com
ISBN 978-1-4258-0472-5
© 2008 Shell Educational Publishing, Inc.

The classroom teacher may reproduce copies of materials in this book for classroom use only. The reproduction of any part for an entire school or school system is strictly prohibited. No part of this publication may be transmitted, stored, or recorded in any form without written permission from the publisher.

Table of Contents

#50472—Greek and Latin Roots © Shell Education

As I began to read this book, the phrase that caught my eye was "divide and conquer." What better way is there to help teachers and students at all grade levels learn how to make sense of difficult, multisyllabic words than by dissecting them? *Greek and Latin Roots: Keys to Building Vocabulary* is a book that does just this. It shows us how to help students understand the meanings of word parts in order to learn new words. This book is an invaluable resource for classroom teachers, content-area teachers, reading specialists, staff developers, curriculum coordinators, and lovers of language. It provides us with important understandings about the English language that most of us did not grow up with and may not have acquired in our schooling.

Did you know that 90 percent of English words with more than one syllable are Latin based and most of the remaining 10 percent are Greek based? Did you know that a single root can help us understand 5–20 related English words? *Greek and Latin Roots: Keys to Building Vocabulary* is packed with this kind of information. Because the English language and the content areas contain so many multisyllabic and technical words, teachers of language arts, science, social studies, and mathematics will find this book particularly helpful in supporting their students as they learn to discern word meanings.

Several aspects of this easy-to-read book also caught my eye, making it a valuable addition to my teaching library. First, it provides a synopsis of the theory and research that support teaching multi-syllabic words by dissecting roots (prefixes, bases, and suffixes). Second, the book offers ideas for planning vocabulary instruction and includes activities like Word Spokes, Wordo, Scattergories, and Making and Writing Words to engage students in actively understanding roots as they become independent word learners. Third, the book includes valuable resources such as extensive lists of commonly taught roots and their meanings, professional resources for teachers, websites, dictionaries, and sources for lesson plans. Finally, as I stopped to reflect at the end of each chapter, it occurred to me that this book is a good resource for a teachers' study group. It is well worth the time spent reading and discussing with colleagues because the ideas it holds are basic to rethinking and transforming vocabulary instruction.

The information in *Greek and Latin Roots: Keys to Building Vocabulary* is critical to being a good vocabulary teacher at all grade levels. I believe the authors have written a terrific book that can help classroom teachers, content-area teachers, reading specialists, staff developers, curriculum coordinators, and lovers of language as they support students in learning how to "divide and conquer" multi-syllabic words.

Karen Bromley, Ph.D.
Distinguished Teaching Professor
School of Education
Binghamton University
State University of New York

Near the end of each calendar year, *Time* magazine has an issue of "10 bests"—news stories, photographs, books, movies, and so on. According to the article written by Gilbert Cruz, one of the "10 Best Buzzwords of 2007" was **locavore** (LO-kuh-vor).

What do you think a *locavore** is? What clues are you using to figure it out?

Most teachers we know find these word puzzles intriguing. We recognize that our language is constantly changing. We spend at least some time thinking about words—which words to teach; how best to teach them; how to assess students' word knowledge; and the relationship between word learning, reading comprehension, and content learning.

It has become increasingly clear in the past couple of decades that a focus on vocabulary has the potential to support much of the other learning students do in school. Yet teachers' questions about how to develop an effective vocabulary program abound. We have all experienced the dreaded vocabulary list approach, complete with writing and memorizing (only to quickly forget) dictionary definitions. We know that this approach doesn't work, but what does?

This is why we wrote this book. In it, you will find research-based practices that can help your students develop their vocabularies. Throughout, we emphasize using word roots (prefixes, suffixes, bases) as an efficient and effective way to build vocabulary. Our instructional series *Building Vocabulary from Word Roots* details year-long word-learning routines for students. In this book, we elaborate on the research and expert opinions supporting this approach to word learning and develop the rationale for focusing on roots in your vocabulary program. This book also provides guidelines for developing models and strategies for vocabulary instruction from a roots perspective, including sample practice activities and stories from teachers who are finding success with this approach to word learning. We also present tips for enhancing your use of a dictionary in the classroom, a brief history of the English language, and an appendix with resources for further learning. Also included in the appendices is a list of commonly taught roots, a list of words with origins in other parts of the world, and suggestions for professional development.

At the conclusion of each chapter, we suggest that you reflect on what you have learned and make notes for your own reference. If you are reading this book with colleagues, you may also want to make note of items for discussion with others.

If you are using *Building Vocabulary from Word Roots* in your classroom, this book will provide you with rationales and adaptations that you and your students may find beneficial. If you are using another vocabulary series (or none at all), this book will provide a background against which you can evaluate your current program or develop a new one. Happy reading!

Timothy Rasinski, Nancy Padak, Evangeline Newton, and Rick M. Newton

* **locavore** (n.)—a person who tries to eat only foods that are harvested locally

Chapter 1

Teaching Vocabulary: What Does the Research Say?

Have you ever visited the National World War II Museum in New Orleans? It is a fascinating place. Among the documents available for viewing is the first draft of President Franklin Delano Roosevelt's famous speech that begins, "Yesterday, December 7, 1941—a date which will live in *infamy*...." These powerful words helped the nation prepare for war. But they were not the first words FDR wrote. The first draft of the beginning of the speech reads, "a date which will live in *world history*." Which do you think is more memorable, "infamy" or "world history"?

Word choice really does make a difference. Samuel Clemens (Mark Twain) once observed that "the difference between the almost right word and the right word is really a large matter—it's the difference between the lightning bug and the lightning." This book is all about helping students find the right word.

As every teacher knows, this is no small task. The English language has between 1,200,000 and 2,000,000 words! And every year, technological advances bring us new modes of communication—and new words. One estimate is that technology is contributing about 20,000 words per year to our language. How can we—and our students—ever catch up? Luckily, there is a way.

Consider this: 90 percent of English words with more than one syllable are Latin based. Most of the remaining 10 percent are Greek based. A single Latin root generates 5–20 English words.

According to Graves and Fitzgerald (2006), school texts and reading materials include more than 180,000 different words. Since most of the words found in these texts come to English from Latin and Greek roots, knowledge of these word parts is a powerful tool in unlocking the complex vocabulary of math, science, literature, and social studies. In addition, most of those 20,000 new "technology" words we mentioned are derived from Latin or Greek. Did you know, for example, that a computer *cursor* and a race *course* both come from the Latin verb *curro*, "to run"?

Today many students come to our classrooms speaking first languages—like Spanish—that are largely derived from Latin. In fact, about 75 percent of the Spanish language is descended from Latin (Chandler and Schwartz 1961). Students who come to school with Spanish as a first language can easily make connections between Spanish and English because the two languages share many cognate words (i.e., words with a common origin). Building vocabulary by learning how to apply the meaning of Latin and Greek word roots can help students who are learning English, as well as others.

Moreover, using roots to unlock word meanings will do more than expand students' vocabularies. Each word built from roots has taken a unique path into our language. Did you know, for example, that the words *vocabulary* and *vowel* come from the Latin root *voc*, which means "voice"? In ancient Rome, students were required to recite lists of new words orally, or using their "voices." And, of course, we need our "voices" to say "a, e, i, o, u." Studying word roots may start your students on a fascinating exploration of word histories. Just as important, it will help students grasp an essential linguistic principle: English words have a discernible logic because their meanings are historically grounded. This knowledge, used in conjunction with word analysis skills, empowers students as learners.

Although no single approach to vocabulary development has been found conclusively to be more successful than another, researchers agree that a focus on Greek and Latin derivatives offers a powerful tool for teachers to nurture students' vocabulary development (Bear, Invernizzi, Templeton, and Johnston 2000; Blachowicz and Fisher 2002, 2006; Newton and Newton 2005; Newton, Padak, and Rasinski 2008; Rasinski and Padak 2001; Stahl 1986, 1992). This is what this book is all about. In this first chapter, we begin our study of roots by addressing two broad and critical issues: why vocabulary is important and what we know about effective instruction. We will then offer some insights into vocabulary instruction for English language learners.

Importance of Vocabulary in Literacy Development

Vocabulary is knowledge of word meanings. The simplicity of this definition does not quite convey what it means to "know" a word. For example, *Merriam-Webster's Collegiate Dictionary* lists 18 definitions (several of them with subdefinitions) for the word *place*. Although we rarely stop to think about it, the issue of knowing words is complex.

Nagy and Scott (2000) have helped us understand the complexity of what it means to know a word. They argue that word knowledge has at least five different components or aspects:

- **Incrementality**—Each time we encounter a new word, our knowledge of its definition(s) and possible uses becomes a bit more precise. Think about how your own understanding of familiar words like *love* or *free* has deepened over time. As Pearson, Hiebert, and Kamil note, "Knowing a word is not an all-or-nothing matter" (2007, 286).

- **Multidimensionality**—Word knowledge extends beyond simple definitions. It can include subtle conceptual differences between synonyms. For example, both *allege* and *believe* share a core meaning of "certainty" or "conviction." Yet they are conceptually distinct. I may "believe" I saw a flying saucer in the sky, but if I report it to the police, they will probably call my sighting an "alleged" event. Why? How are the two words different? Collocation, or the frequent placing together of words, is also a part of word knowledge. We can talk about a *storm front*, but not a *storm back* (Pearson et al. 2007). Similarly, we can have a *storm door* and a *storm window*, but not a *storm ceiling* or a *storm floor*.

- **Polysemy**—Many words, especially common ones, have multiple meanings. Knowing those multiple meanings is part of knowing the words. Think about the different contexts and ways in which the word *place* can be used. An outdoor grocery store can be called a *marketplace*, while a horse who *places* comes in second in a race. And remember Dorothy in *The Wizard of Oz*? She reminded us that "there's no *place* like home."

- **Interrelatedness**—Knowing a word often involves knowing its attributes and how it is related to other words or concepts. Think of all the things you know about even a simple concept like *cat*, and you will quickly see this aspect of interrelatedness in action.

- **Heterogeneity**—A word's meaning is dependent on its context, both semantic and syntactic. Again using *place* as an example, consider:

  - Her ideas were all over the place.
  - In gym we had to run in place.
  - This weekend we will go to our summer place.

There is nothing simple about knowing a word. As Pearson et al. note, "Words may seem like simple entities, but they are not. Their surface simplicity belies a deeper complexity" (2007, 286).

Thinking about the word knowledge that students bring to the classroom adds another layer of complexity. For example, each of us has an active vocabulary and a passive vocabulary. An active vocabulary includes words we can quickly generate for speaking or writing because we know them well. We can recognize words in our passive vocabulary when we encounter them, but we don't regularly use them. Think back to FDR's speech. Chances are we understood what FDR meant by "infamy" because we have seen it in other contexts. Yet, when is the last time you used this word in a sentence? One goal of vocabulary instruction is to increase both active and passive vocabularies. This goal is critical because research has shown that students who begin school with smaller vocabularies remain at an academic disadvantage throughout their schooling (Hart and Risley 1995, 2003).

The social context in which words are encountered provides yet another layer of complexity. We use oral vocabulary to listen and speak, and print vocabulary to read and write. Spoken language is socially contextualized. In conversation, for example, we use gestures to help convey meaning. The participants in a conversation can ask for clarification. Written language, on the other hand, tends to be socially decontextualized, so precision of word choice is very important. No one is easily available to clarify a text's meaning. Most of the new vocabulary students encounter in school is through reading written texts, and much of it is decontextualized.

Decades of research have consistently found a deep connection between vocabulary knowledge, reading comprehension, and academic success (Baumann, Kameenui, and Ash 2003). Kamil and Hiebert describe vocabulary as a bridge between the "word-level processes of phonics and the cognitive processes of comprehension" (2005, 4). This is a useful way to visualize the importance of vocabulary for young readers. A solid bank of conceptual knowledge is essential for reading because it facilitates word identification and enables comprehension. But meaning does not automatically follow successful decoding. If a word is not in a child's oral vocabulary, the child cannot apply word recognition strategies effectively, and reading comprehension is hindered (National Reading Panel [NRP] 2000). Wide conceptual knowledge supports decoding. An extensive vocabulary helps students read fluently, comprehend, discuss what they have read, and learn. Another goal of vocabulary instruction, then, is to expand students' conceptual knowledge.

The decontextualized language of school texts contains richer vocabulary and more unfamiliar words than spoken language (Cunningham 2005). In addition to enhancing students' oral and written vocabularies for general conversation or writing, students also need to learn the infrequently used words that will help them comprehend their increasingly complex school texts. Thus, students need multiple opportunities to experience words in both oral and written contexts to expand their conceptual knowledge. You may agree with us that this is a daunting task. For example, although most researchers believe that students naturally add between 2,000 and 3,000 new words each year, Nagy and Anderson (1984) estimate that fifth graders encounter 10,000 new words each year in their reading alone.

Fortunately, 4,000 of the 10,000 new words that fifth graders encounter are derivatives of familiar words, most of them of Latin or Greek origin (usually compound words and words with prefixes and suffixes). In fact, well over half of English words—nearly 75 percent according to some estimates—are derived from Greek or Latin. This is why a focus on word parts makes sense as part of a vocabulary program.

The "Roots Advantage"

Latin and Greek prefixes, bases, and suffixes are fairly consistent in their meanings and spelling patterns. Consequently, students can figure out the pronunciation and meaning of many new words by looking at their roots. They will understand the logic in the spelling pattern. A student who knows that the root *spec* means "look," for example, has a head start in figuring out what *speculate*, *spectacular*, and *spectacle* mean when encountering them in a text. The student can then use context to determine whether the *spectacle* in question is a "big event" or, when used in the plural form, a "pair of glasses." This clear link among pronunciation, meaning, and spelling is especially useful for young readers because they are able to coordinate sound and sense when they encounter new and challenging words (Bear et al. 2000; Rasinski and Padak 2001).

Through each passing year, students encounter more and more words of classical origin. As they move from grade to grade, students face an increased number of "new words, new concepts, and multiple meanings" (Blachowicz and Fisher 2002, 511). Most new school vocabulary is found in content-area textbooks, which adds unique challenges because learning new words in content areas often requires learning new concepts as well. Most content-area words are "low-frequency" and "do not appear in other contexts" (Harmon, Hedrick, and Wood 2005, 263). Furthermore, the same words may represent dissimilar concepts in different content areas: consider a *revolution* in history, for example, and the *revolution* of Earth around the sun. In addition, key content-area vocabulary is often a building block for more advanced conceptual knowledge. Unlike primary-level students who can use context to determine the general meaning of a word, older students must learn new conceptual vocabulary with enough precision to scaffold other concepts.

We hope that this brief research review has convinced you that effective vocabulary instruction with Latin and Greek roots has the potential to foster students' literacy learning. Unfortunately, at present there is little classroom-based research that provides descriptions of effective vocabulary instruction in practice. Sweet and Snow (2003), reporting on results from the RAND Reading Study Group's examination of comprehension, note that the number of studies examining the effect of vocabulary instruction on reading comprehension has been small. Similarly, the NRP noted that research on vocabulary acquisition greatly "exceeds current knowledge of pedagogy" and cited a "great need" for research on this topic "in authentic school contexts, with real teachers, under real conditions" (2000, 4–4).

Despite the current lack of research, however, the need for comprehensive vocabulary curricula is apparent (Blachowicz,

Fisher, Ogle, and Watts-Taffe 2006). In the next section, we offer general principles for designing vocabulary instruction.

Five Principles for Word Learning

Until recently, most formal vocabulary instruction has been limited to the introduction of key words before reading a new text. Yet the NRP (2000) found that vocabulary is learned both indirectly and directly, and that dependence on only one instructional method does not result in optimal vocabulary growth. The NRP report also affirmed early research that identified readers' vocabularies as a powerful predictor of successful reading (Davis 1944).

Although researchers agree on the curricular importance of vocabulary instruction, guidance about instructional methodology is still in early stages. Kamil and Hiebert (2005) identify four core unresolved instructional issues that have serious implications for lesson planning: 1) how many words should be taught; 2) which words should be taught; 3) how we should teach students for whom reading is difficult and/or English is a second language; and 4) how independent reading supports vocabulary learning.

Despite these ongoing issues, researchers are beginning to provide instructional guidance in vocabulary acquisition. For example, Biemiller argues that even different student populations learn words "largely in the same order" and calls for teaching a corpus of common word roots, even in primary grades (2005, 225). Blachowicz and Fisher believe that two decades of research on vocabulary acquisition can be summarized into four broad instructional principles: Students should 1) engender an "understanding of words and ways to learn them" through active engagement; 2) "personalize" word learning; 3) be "immersed" in words; and 4) experience "repeated exposures" by accessing words through "multiple sources of information" (2002, 504).

Researchers also agree that no single instructional method is sufficient to enhance students' vocabularies. Teachers need a variety of methods that teach word meanings while increasing the depth of word knowledge (Blachowicz et al. 2006; Lehr, Osborn, and Hiebert 2007). The following principles can be used to select, evaluate, or create effective vocabulary instruction:

1. Instruction should include *planned teaching* of selected words with multiple kinds of information provided (e.g., semantic, structural) (Blachowicz et al. 2006). Research tells us that students can only learn 8–10 new words each week through direct instruction (Stahl and Fairbanks 1986). Some direct instruction is useful.

2. Vocabulary instruction should be *integrative* (Nagy 1988). To learn new words—really learn them—requires students to connect new and existing knowledge. Words are best learned when presented meaningfully with attention to definitions (Nagy 1988; Stahl 1986). Students need to use new words in meaningful contexts and think about them in meaningful ways. Attention to definitions adds power to this word learning (Stahl and Fairbanks 1986). Teachers must find ways to focus on connections between what students already know and words they are going to learn. Activities that ask students to explore similarities and differences among concepts, activate background knowledge, and generate and test hypotheses seem particularly beneficial (Blachowicz and Fisher 2002; Marzano, Pickering, and Pollock 2001).

3. Vocabulary instruction needs to include repetition (Blachowicz and Fisher 2002; Nagy 1988; Stahl 1986). Students should be *immersed* in words, with frequent opportunities to use new words in diverse oral and print contexts in order to learn them on a deep level. Research tells us that we learn more new words incidentally, when they occur in our reading or listening, than we do through direct instruction (Lehr et al. 2007). In other words, looking up words in a dictionary and learning definitions are not enough to ensure word learning. We need to do more.

Teacher read-alouds can help students develop vocabulary, especially if read-aloud books have wonderful words and powerful language. If students will be tackling a new or difficult concept in the content areas, read-alouds could include picture books or other texts that address the topic. Related to this principle is another: the importance of students' wide reading. The more students read, the better. Using new words in discussion and writing also facilitates their learning. In fact, we recommend that you challenge students to use new words in as many ways as possible.

4. Word learning is a procedural activity—a matter of knowing *how*. Therefore, *students need strategies* for determining word meaning (Nagy and Scott 2000). Students need to understand and know how to manipulate the structural features of language. Most vocabulary-related school tasks naively presume this kind of knowledge. Classroom-based studies have demonstrated the effectiveness of two strategies that are particularly important for vocabulary development: teaching context clues and word parts (Baumann, Font, Edwards, and Boland 2005).

Context clues are frequently used as a reading strategy for determining the meaning of an unknown word. Although context in reading has many dimensions, it most often refers to figuring out the meaning of an unknown word by getting help (or clues) from the words, phrases, sentences, or illustrations surrounding it (Harris and Hodges 1995). The help that context provides may be semantic, based on the meaning of the surrounding words or sentences. It may also be structural, based on grammatical or syntactic markers within a word or sentence.

Using context clues is an especially important strategy for vocabulary development because, as we noted earlier, many English words have multiple meanings. Since context is crucial in identifying which meaning to use, learning how to use the surrounding context helps students expand their vocabularies.

Morphological analysis, another important strategy, allows students to make connections among semantically related words or word families (Nagy and Scott 2000). By separating and analyzing the meaning of a prefix, suffix, or other word root, students can often unlock the meaning of an unknown word. If we teach students that *bi-* means "two," for example, they can use that information to figure out *biannual* or *biaxial*. When introducing the concept of *photosynthesis*, we can easily point out its roots: *photo* means "light," and *syn* means "with." As students grapple with the complex process of how light (*photo*) is combined with (*syn*) carbon dioxide and water to make sugar, knowledge of these word roots will support their efforts.

Knowing that words can be broken down into units of meaning is a powerful strategy for vocabulary development. Until recently, teaching word roots was a strategy reserved for upper-grade or content-area classrooms. But a growing body of research tells us that this strategy should be introduced early. In fact, by the second grade, students should be adept at using word roots as a vocabulary strategy (Biemiller 2005). Learning key word parts will enable students to understand new words that are semantically connected. In this way, instruction becomes efficient—by learning one word part, students have clues to the meaning of all the words that contain it.

5. Vocabulary instruction must foster *word consciousness*, an awareness of and interest in words (Graves and Watts-Taffe 2002). Activities like word exploration (e.g., etymology) and word play (e.g., puns and riddles) are central to vocabulary development. Moreover, they provide pleasant ways to accomplish the repetition necessary for students to learn new words.

Dictionaries and other reference works can add interest to a vocabulary program. Although most students begin to learn about reference tools in the primary grades, they may not know the enormous variety of electronic and print dictionaries now available. They may know the concepts of synonym and antonym, but they may not know how to use a thesaurus. (Some of the electronic ones available are really fun to use! The last chapter of this book contains Web addresses for some of our favorite online reference sites.) Practice with reference tools will help students learn to use them automatically. A vocabulary program should encourage students to become word sleuths, a habit that they may well carry with them throughout (and beyond) their school years.

You can also share your own love of words. Each of us has favorite texts that we turn to because the words move us to laughter or tears. Reading these texts aloud to students and talking about the power of words is an effective practice. You can also whet students' appetites by sharing interesting word histories and then showing students how to explore the origins of words themselves. Posting lists of websites or print resources for students to investigate can help make word learning and word play a priority in the classroom as well.

Words themselves are just plain interesting, and our ultimate goal is to create lifelong word lovers. Crossword puzzles, word scrambles, riddles, and tongue twisters are fun, but they're also good vocabulary practice. Make time for students to play and explore word games on their own or with others.

Vocabulary Development for English Language Learners

Students learning English as a second (or additional) language have unique advantages as well as unique challenges. Their rich background experiences can be tapped to enhance everyone's learning. They know how to move between two languages, integrating sounds and meanings into new words and grammatical structures. Their natural manipulation of two languages promotes higher-level thinking. Yet they sometimes feel lost in the unfamiliar linguistic and academic world in which they find themselves. And research has shown us that learning English vocabulary is a crucial task for English language learners (Nation 2001).

Becoming literate in a second language can take five to seven years, depending on the speaker's proficiency with his or her first language, the type of second-language instruction, and how much English the student knows at the time instruction begins (Perez 2004). The beginning of this process can be worrisome for teachers: "Most new English language learners will go through a silent period during which they are unable or unwilling to communicate orally in the new language" (Haynes 2007, 9). Yet at every stage of learning English, instruction can support students' learning.

Fortunately, everything we know about how to teach vocabulary applies to both first- and second-language learners: English language learners need to focus on meaning by using research-based strategies to learn new words. They need frequent opportunities to try out new words in varied learning contexts. The major difference is that English language learners generally require more distinctive scaffolding. Two ideas will help you plan vocabulary instruction for English language learners:

- Use discussion to support word learning. Discussion opportunities benefit English language learners by supporting their growth in conversational English, as well as by promoting word learning. Students don't simply "soak up" language. They need comprehensible input— slightly above their current language level—that builds on prior knowledge. They also need lots of opportunities to practice, especially in small-group settings (Haynes 2007; Perez 2004).

- Use students' native languages (or references to their native languages) whenever possible. Many English words have cognates in other languages. Spanish-speaking students can easily relate many new English words to Spanish because they share Latin derivatives. In teaching *aqueduct*, for example, students may already have the concept of "water" from the Spanish word *agua*. Encourage students to draw such connections between their first and second languages.

Summary

We have presented a research-based rationale for addressing vocabulary in your classroom, five guiding principles that you can use to develop an instructional curriculum, and a few ideas about adaptations that may support English language learners. We wish you success in your word journeys. In the end, we hope you and your students will agree with British novelist Evelyn Waugh:

"One forgets words as one forgets names. One's vocabulary needs constant fertilizing or it will die."

Chapter 2

A Root Awakening

In the first chapter of this book, we discussed the importance of vocabulary in students' literacy development. We saw a direct link between our students' vocabularies and their prospects for academic success. We noted that as students advance through school, research indicates that they encounter increasingly more complex words and concepts (Blachowicz and Fisher 2002). Only those students who have mastered the conceptual, or content, vocabulary at a lower level are well equipped to unlock the meanings of academic words, particularly in the content areas.

It is clear, then, that knowing how to unlock the meaning of new words is an important lifelong skill for our students and for us. Understanding how words work shows us how to think in new ways about words—those we already know and those that are new to us. In this chapter, we present some useful strategies and rationale for teaching vocabulary from a roots perspective. Then we explain the strategy of Divide and Conquer, introducing the three kinds of roots. But first, what is a root?

What Is a Root?

Words, like stories, have a structure. We all know that most good stories have a beginning, middle, and end, and that these parts of stories connect with one another. Each part has a purpose and advances the overall story line. When we read and discuss stories with our students, we often ask, "What happens in this part of the story?" "What if this part of the story had been different?" "What happened before this part?" Depending on the length of the story, we learn to identify its different parts as chapters, as pages with headings, as paragraphs, as sentences, and so on. In order to understand a story, we often take it apart so that we can think and talk about all the things that occur in the beginning, middle, and end of the plot. When our students create their own stories, we encourage them to think and compose in terms of these manageable and meaningful parts.

Likewise, many English words—and nearly all the academic words our students must learn—are made up of parts. Like the parts of a story, the parts of a word also carry meaning. And this is precisely what a word root is: a part of a word that carries meaning. Think about this for a moment before moving ahead. A word is composed, of course, of letters. But letters, by themselves, carry only sound, not meaning. The letter *r*, for example, has no meaning by itself. It's a sound, nothing more and nothing less. Letters, then, are word parts, but they are not roots because they have no meaning.

Similarly, the phonemes that students learn to recognize in primary grades are associated with letters or letter combinations that produce sound, but not meaning. As very young children learn to read and write, for example, they learn to recognize the phoneme *an* in such words as *fan, man, can, dandy, sand, dancer*, and *ran*. These words share a phoneme and sound alike, to be sure, but they have no shared meaning. It is important for beginning readers to develop fluency in recognizing letters and sound units because this enables them to hear and readily understand the words they see on a printed page. But this skill enables them to read and spell only the words they already know. In other words, a correctly decoded or pronounced word is understandable only when they already know what it means. Thus, even a full knowledge of letters and phonemes does not generate growth in vocabulary or word comprehension. A student may know 100 words with the phoneme *an* and still be at a loss when encountering such new words as *phantom, sanitize*, and *tantrum*. The student may be able to sound out these words, but the sounds generate no conceptual awareness. The sounds alone do not lead the student to the meaning of the new word. From the phoneme, the student gets the sound but not the sense. However, teaching phonemes and word families do set the foundation for teaching students to look for word parts. This shows students how knowing a word part can lead to knowing other words. And, it develops automatically with simple words that allow students to fully concentrate on the harder multisyllabic words of academic and content-specific vocabulary.

Now, compare a phoneme with a word root. Remember how we defined *root* above: a word part that carries meaning. To be a bit more precise: a word root is a semantic unit. This simply means that a root is a word part that means something. It is a group of letters with meaning. A phoneme, by contrast, is a word part that carries only sound. When a root appears inside a word, it lends its meaning to the word and thus helps create the word's meaning. Moreover, words that contain the same root also share meaning. We call these related words cognates (from Latin *cognatus*, which means "born together, related in origin"). Notice how different this is from a phoneme, which only enables us to pronounce words. Like a phoneme, a root is also a group of letters. But unlike the phoneme, the root conveys not only sound but also meaning.

One of the most commonly encountered roots in English words, for example, is *mot*. The root *mot* is not a word in itself, but it is more than a phoneme because *mot* means something; it is a semantic unit. This particular root means "move." Nearly any time it appears in a word, that word will have a meaning associated with movement. Take a minute to think of *mot* words that have to do with movement—or better yet, ask your students to do so! In a short time, even the youngest students will be able to generate a list that can be written on the board:

- A *motor* makes things move.
- A *motorcycle* moves down the street.
- A *locomotive* moves on tracks.
- Some outdoor lights are triggered by *motion* detectors.
- Some classrooms have a lot of *commotion*.
- We all were *promoted* last year and moved ahead to the next grade.
- Who lost the *remote control* to the television?

By drawing a box around or otherwise highlighting the root that all these words share (*mot*), you can give your students a "root awakening": Words with a shared root have a shared meaning. They are cognates.

Why Teach Roots?

Many primary-grade students will be familiar with most, if not all, of the *mot* words in the above list. They will all have some awareness of *motors, motorcycles, locomotives, school promotions,* and—as any classroom teacher can attest to—*commotion*. These are familiar words and concepts, and by bringing them together in this way, students quickly come to understand the linguistic principle that words with the same roots are related in meaning.

Beyond this, teaching the meaning of a root like *mot* equips students to build new *mot* words and expand their vocabularies. For example, you can write some of the following words or phrases on the board and ask students to figure out the "movement" in their shared meanings:

- What *motivated* you to do that?
- What were your *motives* for saying this?
- What *emotions* did you feel when you learned the news?
- What is a *motif* in music?
- Do *promotion* gimmicks really work?
- Who wants to make a *motion* that we end this meeting?
- My brother was *demoted* because of his unruly conduct.
- Why is it hard to get to *remote* locations?

With the roots approach to vocabulary learning, students discover how to look for meaningful connections between words they already know (like *motor*) and words that they may not know (like *motif*), as well as with words they may have heard before but only vaguely know (like *demotion* or *motivate*). This discovery may also bring them a deeper understanding of a familiar word. Can you figure out the "movement" in *emotion*? When we teach vocabulary based on roots rather than word lists, we encourage our students to search for a word's meaning from the meaning of its root. By associating these words with their cognates, students become word sleuths as they ask questions about meaning and then try to answer them.

One way to help students think through and unlock the meaning of a word based on its root is to reword the sentence substituting the root meaning for the word. "What *motivated* you to do that?" can be translated as "What *moved* you to do that?" Another way is to define the word using the root meaning. A self-*motivated* student is a "self-starter" who "moves" on his or her own to learn. In fact, we often refer to someone with such energy as a "mover and a shaker." Similarly, our *motives* are the forces that "move" us to do or say certain things.

The possibilities are endless! Students will enjoy puzzling through some of the more challenging cognates. A *motif* in music is a theme or refrain that "moves" from part to part in the overall composition. When we hear a *motif* in one part of the symphony, we may hear it repeated in a different key in a later movement. A *motif* in a novel is a theme that "moves" around the story, cropping up here and there.

Applying root definitions also deepens students' understanding of a word's multiple meanings and introduces them to new usages. All students know that being *promoted* means advancing to the next grade (*pro-* = "forward"). Asking students to consider other kinds of "forward movement" will get them to consider additional dimensions: A store needs to "move" its products "forward" in the market in order to sell more of them. Moreover, if a *promotion* is a "moving forward," then a *demotion* must be a "moving downward" to a lower grade or lower status. Even our *emotions* can be understood as feelings that "move" us. When we feel sad and cry, we might say we have been "moved" to tears. When our *emotions* are aroused, we might say we feel deeply "moved." And there is even movement when someone makes a *motion* in a business meeting. If the motion is seconded, the chairperson of the meeting then says, "It has been *moved* and seconded that…."

In our first chapter, we mentioned that the same words can mean different things in different contexts. Confusion often results when a student learns a word as having one meaning, only to learn later that it can mean something else. A *promotion* to a higher grade in school is not the same thing as a sales *promotion*. But in either context, *promotion* retains its basic meaning of the "movement" of something or someone ahead. This root-level awareness of words can be a real boon to our students. Let's consider the word *remote*. Most students will readily know what a *remote control* device is: it allows us to change television channels without getting out of our chairs. We use a *remote control* device when we are at a distance, or "removed" from, the TV. When the context changes and we later read or hear about a *remote* location, we can activate our students' background knowledge by asking them to associate the known concept of "remote control" with the new concept of a "remote location." By talking about these two contexts that share the same word, we can guide our students to a root-level understanding. A remote control is far away from the TV, and a remote location is far away from most people.

In the previous chapter, we observed that students can learn only 8–10 new words per week through direct instruction. But we have just identified more than a dozen words that come from the root *mot*. By learning just one root, students can easily add between 10 and 20 connected words.

Increasing Word Awareness

In Chapter 1, we talked about the need to build students' active and passive vocabularies. Most roots generate everyday words that students readily understand and actively use; however, the same roots also generate newer and harder content words that will expand students' passive vocabularies. This is critically important to success in school because most of the texts students encounter rely heavily on technical or complex vocabulary that most of our students do not use in daily conversation. When we teach roots, we reinforce the vocabulary that students have already acquired and then build on that reinforced foundation. The roots approach activates background knowledge and encourages students to advance from the known to the unknown.

Think back to our discussion of the root *mot*. Did you notice how easy it was to understand the root meaning of "move"? Roots have base-level meanings that are not conceptually difficult. They refer to essential things and actions that all language speakers understand. Because roots tend to have basic meanings, they enable us to understand even difficult words. When we divide and conquer, we simplify and open the door to understanding. Because everyone knows what *movement* is, students can easily establish a connection between the movement of a motorcycle and the more sophisticated movement and motif of a symphony.

One final observation on the root *mot*. In the first chapter, we noted that with continuing advances in technology, the English language will continue to add vocabulary of a scholarly, scientific, and technical nature. Think of the phrase *remote control*, which came into existence only after the invention of electricity. The new device needed a new word, and we created one from the appropriate root. Now in the computer age, we find the same root *mot* in its newest form. The smiley faces that show up on our computer screens are cleverly called *emoticons*. This new word, found only in the most recent of dictionaries, is composed of word parts that have meaning. An emoticon is an *icon* (an image) viewed on a computer screen that indicates a particular *emotion*. As vocabulary is born to give names to new things and concepts, Latin and Greek roots remain the foundation of our English language. In fact, if we know our roots, we can "divide and conquer" all the new vocabulary that the twenty-first century will bring!

Roots are found in vocabulary from all phases of life. Seeing the world of words from a roots perspective fosters word awareness, the ultimate goal of all vocabulary programs. It can be eye-opening for a third grader, for example, to "divide and conquer" a school word like *promotion* and connect it with a mundane word like *motor*. Years later, the same student may be playing in a school band and quickly recognize a musical *motif* as coming from the same root as *promotion*. Like a motif in a lifelong symphony of learning, roots keep returning to us in new contexts. And roots, once learned, are rarely forgotten. Knowledge of roots will help your students throughout their lives engage in conceptual thinking about the fundamental meanings of words and the varieties of ways in which they can be used.

The Three Kinds of Roots

Roman military leader Julius Caesar famously wrote, "All Gaul is divided into three parts." Like a military general, we can employ the Divide and Conquer strategy. Many English words can also be divided into three parts:

- the prefix

- the base

- the suffix

Prefixes, bases, and suffixes are the three kinds of roots, or semantic units, found in many words. Although sometimes the words *root* and *base* are used the same way, they are not interchangeable. *Root* is the generic term for any part of a word that holds meaning (Ayers 1986). Prefixes, bases, and suffixes are kinds of roots. In terms of a word's structure, the prefix appears at the beginning of a word, the base in the middle, and the suffix at the end. This umbrella diagram helps illustrate the distinctions between a prefix, base, and suffix:

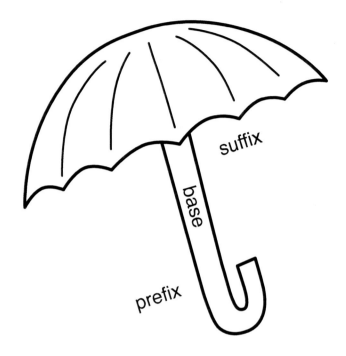

Roots, then, is the umbrella term for the subcategories of prefix, base, and suffix. Notice that the *base* in this picture is shown as the handle of the umbrella. The base holds up the entire word, providing its essential or "basic" meaning.

What Does a Base Do?

The root *mot* is a base that means "move." Here are a few more examples of bases:

- *tract* = "pull, draw, drag"
- *duc, duct* = "lead"
- *port* = "carry"
- *ven, vent* = "come"
- *dic, dict* = "speak"
- *voc, vok* = "call"

- *viv, vit* = "life"
- *sol, helio* = "sun"
- *dom* = "house"
- *terra* = "land"
- *aqua, hydro* = "water"

These bases generate entire words that carry their basic meanings:

- A *motor* makes things "move."
- *Motion* is "movement."
- A *tractor* "pulls" farm equipment.
- We need good *traction* to "pull" a car through ice or snow.
- When we *trace* something, we make a "drawing."
- A *duct* "leads" heated air from a furnace to the rooms of the house.
- A *porter* "carries" luggage.
- A *portable* television can be "carried" from one room to another.

Notice that each of the italicized words in the above list has a meaning directly associated with the meaning of the base itself. In fact, the base *duct* can even function as a whole word all by itself! And as we noted earlier, these bases carry fundamental, easily understood meanings: move, pull or drag, lead, and carry. You may have noticed that none of the words in this particular list begins with a prefix. The first semantic unit in these words is the base itself.

What Does a Prefix Do?

When a prefix is attached to the base of a word, the prefix does one of three things: it gives a word direction, negates a word by meaning "not," or intensifies the meaning of a word by adding the notion of "very." For this reason, we speak of three categories of prefixes:

- directional prefixes
- negative prefixes
- intensifying prefixes

Most of the prefixes found in English words—about 25 in all—are derived from Latin. Teaching the meaning of prefixes is especially helpful to young children because a few prefixes are used in a large number of words. Moreover, nine prefixes account for 75 percent of the words that use prefixes (White, Sowell, and Yanagihara 1989).

Prefixes appear with such frequency in our vocabularies that students can easily learn some of them just by recalling words they already know. For example, every school has *exit* signs that point to the way "out of" the building. You can use this everyday word to teach that the prefix *ex-* sometimes means the direction "out, out of." *Ex-* can have an intensifying meaning as well. For example, an *exhausted* person is "very" drained (*haust* = "drain"). Another example of an intensifying prefix is the *per-* in *perfection*, "made well" (*fect* = "make, do"). Many students will have seen a band or orchestra *conductor* wave a baton, leading musicians "together" as they play their instruments. You can use this familiar concept to teach that the prefix *con-* is a directional prefix meaning "with, together." When we tell students to *redo* an assignment, they know they must go "back" and do it "again." You can use this school experience to teach that *re-* is a directional prefix meaning "back, again." A student who is *unable* to come to a birthday party is "not" able to do so: *un-* is a negative prefix. Likewise, *in-*, *im-*, and *il-* are negating prefixes. Consider words like *invisible*, *impossible*, and *illegal*.

Most of the prefixes students encounter in school texts are directional in nature. This means that they indicate a path of some kind: "with, together," "under," "in," "out," "back, again," "away from," "out of." Here are a few examples of the most common directional prefixes:

- *at-, ad-* = "to, toward, add to"

- *de-* = "down, off"

- *dis-* = "apart, in different directions"

- *con-* = "with, together"

- *ex-* = "out"

- *pro-* = "forward, ahead"

- *sub-* = "under, below"

- *in-* = "in"

Once students have learned the directional meanings of these prefixes, they can generate a large number of words from even a single base. Here are some *tract* ("pull, draw, drag") words with directional prefixes:

- Previews of coming *attractions* "draw" us "to" the theater.

- The ugly building *detracted* ("pulled down") from the beauty of the neighborhood.

- Noises in a school hallway are *distracting* because they "draw" our attention "away" from the lesson.

- Muscles *contract* when they "pull together" and tighten.

- A dentist *extracts* a bad tooth by "pulling" it "out."

- A *protracted* war is one that is "drawn forward."

- When we *subtract*, we "draw" the number "below" its amount by taking away from it.

All of the italicized words above are cognates derived from a single base, *tract*. Each of these words, furthermore, begins with a directional prefix that indicates the direction of the "pulling, drawing, or dragging."

What Does a Suffix Do?

If a word has a suffix, it comes at the end of a word. Unlike prefixes and bases, which have fixed and stable meanings, suffixes have meanings that are fluid. The essential function of a suffix is to indicate the part of speech of a particular word. We speak of noun suffixes, adjectival suffixes, and verbal suffixes. We don't need to teach these grammatical concepts to young children, though. When it comes to understanding what a word means, the suffix is the least important component. By the time students have reflected on the prefix and the base, they usually understand the word well enough to figure it out. None of us thinks explicitly of parts of speech when we speak or write and, thankfully, it is not the purpose of vocabulary instruction to make our students sound like dictionaries as they talk about a word and its range of meanings. Students do not need to give—and often should not be asked to give—dictionary definitions of words. In fact, it can be counterproductive to lock in the meaning of a word with a single definition since words can change meaning when their contexts change. Instead, we should encourage them to use words in a phrase or sample sentence. This way, they will be providing a linguistic context.

The ending of a word, therefore, rarely poses a problem for students. If a student has trouble figuring out a new word, the challenging portions will lie in either the prefix or the base. It is unlikely, for example, that a student with age-appropriate English language skills would refer to a *portable* television (*portable* is an adjective: "able to be" carried) as a *porter* television (*porter* is a noun: "one who" carries luggage). Once the student identifies the base of these words as meaning "carry," he or she is well equipped to deduce the meaning.

For these reasons, the roots approach to vocabulary places an emphasis on prefixes (directional, negative, and intensifying) and bases (the core meaning of the word). Only a few suffixes merit intensive scrutiny. Words of Greek origin, for example, tend to be long and often carry technical meanings. Thus, it can be useful to students to learn that the suffix *-ology* means "study of." By dividing and conquering this suffix, they will be able to think about the base meaning in such words as:

- *Geology* is the "study of" the earth.

- *Theology* is the "study of" God.

- *Hematology* is the "study of" blood.

- *Anthropology* is the "study of" human cultures.

For more discussion on suffixes, see pages 61–64.

Summary

In this chapter, we have addressed some of the basics of word-root study. We have explained what we mean when we speak of roots, and we have offered some compelling reasons for the Divide and Conquer approach to vocabulary instruction as a way to build students' active and passive vocabularies. In the next chapter, we will suggest some instructional basics. We will offer some strategies on how to divide and conquer words and how to "talk around" words in a way that will help students make connections between the new words they are learning and the old or current ones they already know. We will provide more sample roots—prefixes, bases, and suffixes—that teachers can use at various levels in elementary and middle school.

Chapter 3

Planning Vocabulary Instruction

In the first chapters of this book, we built a research-based rationale for the importance of vocabulary instruction. We also explained our focus on word parts (or roots) and offered suggestions about which word parts to use as the basis for instruction. In this chapter, we draw upon all of this background information and focus on ideas for planning vocabulary instruction. First we address instructional basics like time, and how to develop an instructional model. Next we explain several instructional routines; we show them in action using a sample week from *Building Vocabulary from Word Roots*, Level 5 (Rasinski, Padak, Newton, and Newton 2006). Finally we offer some advice about differentiating instruction and assessing students' vocabulary growth.

Instructional Planning: The Basics

Before developing an instructional model, you should consider the issue of time. How much time per day can you devote to vocabulary instruction? Daily attention to vocabulary is important because, as we noted in Chapter 1, "students should be immersed in words, with frequent opportunities to use new words in diverse oral and print contexts in order to learn them on a deep level." Just 10 to 15 minutes focused on vocabulary instruction and guided practice each day will foster this sense of immersion. For your vocabulary program to meet its goals, you need to devote consistent time to it.

We think there are three important points in deciding on an overall instructional model. First you need a routine. Although incidental word learning is important and powerful (NRP 2000), it is not enough. Certainly, occasional "teachable moments" enrich word study. But this hit-or-miss way of working with words cannot, by itself, lead to the deep word learning we seek.

Consider, instead, developing a routine—a consistent block of time "during which a predictable set of activities regularly occur. Routines allow teachers to maximize the amount of time spent on instruction and minimize time spent on giving directions [or] explaining procedures" (Rasinski and Padak 2004, 25). In other words, developing routines will make the best use of your daily 10–15 minute vocabulary session. Students will know what's coming and how to participate effectively. For example, if Divide and Conquer is one of your routines, you won't have to waste time explaining its procedures each time you do it. Instead, students will know how to think about the general concept and can devote their attention to the particular word elements for that lesson.

Routines don't have to be routine. We hope that reading aloud to your students is one of your daily routines, for example. Because you read something new each day, your read-aloud routine isn't routine, but it is predictable. Students know to look forward to it. So it is with vocabulary routines. Students know that they'll be spending time each day thinking about and learning new words. This sends a subtle message about what's important in your classroom—words and vocabulary study.

A second point to consider in developing an overall instructional model can be summarized in two words: teachers teach. Making assignments, monitoring students' activity, and assessing students' work are surely part of your day, but they aren't teaching. Showing, telling, scaffolding, explaining— these teaching actions will enhance your students' vocabulary learning.

A third point to consider is that you base instructional routines on a "gradual release of responsibility" (Weaver 2002). At the beginning, when students need you most, you might lead discussion. Later, as students develop some control over the new learning, small groups or pairs of students working under your guidance can offer the scaffolding students will need to achieve success. Eventually, students can "show what they know" independently. So your goal should be an overall approach that begins with teacher-led discussion followed by activities that scaffold increasingly independent learning.

Recommendations for Instructional Routines

Here are a few recommendations for your instruction: spend about 10–15 minutes each day on vocabulary; make sure your instruction focuses on selected word parts or roots; and gradually release responsibility to the students. With these general ideas as a framework, we now describe several routines that collectively will enable you to achieve your goals for students' word learning.

We recommend that you begin each week (or some other instructional cycle) by inviting students to "meet a root." The root lists provided in Chapter 4, Chapter 7, and Appendix C may help you select a root for focus. If you are using *Building Vocabulary from Word Roots*, we have made these selections for you. The next stage in instructional planning is to develop routines based on this root. We recommend the following: Divide and Conquer, Combine and Create, Read and Reason, Extend and Explore, and Go for the Gold! For example, each routine is explained with reference to instruction that focuses on *stru*, *struct*, which means "build" (Level 5, Unit IV, Lesson 20 of *Building Vocabulary from Word Roots*).

Divide and Conquer

The strategy of Divide and Conquer (word dissection) helps

students see the root in the context of words so that they can learn how to identify it and use its meaning to determine the meaning of an unfamiliar word. With Divide and Conquer, students "get into" words by looking for familiar prefixes and a common base shared by all these words. A short list of cognate words (i.e., words that share a common base) provides a good introduction to this activity. You might start with a list of words like these, which are all built on the Latin bases *stru*, *struct*, which mean "build":

- structure
- construct
- construction
- obstruct
- deconstruct
- infrastructure
- reconstruct

You can begin by activating background knowledge and drawing students' awareness to the everyday occurrence of this root in their existing vocabularies. Most students will know that a *structure* is a building. Many have had to drive through *construction zones* on their way to school in which they saw "building" going on along the roadside. You may show them a piece of *construction paper* and ask them how it differs from regular notebook paper. Construction paper is heavier and stiffer than writing paper because we use it to "build" figures (and not merely to draw on).

You can also activate background knowledge by focusing on the prefixes found in some or all of these words, depending on which ones students know. You can ask them to talk about these words and use the meaning of the base (they should say "build" in their responses) and the meaning of the prefix (*con-* = "with, together"; *de-* = "down, off"; *re-* = "back, again"). So, they may come up with the following suggestions: When we *construct* things, we put a lot of different parts [bricks, cement, wood] "together" and "build" them. When they *deconstruct* a building, they knock the "building" "down." When we *reconstruct* something, we "build" it "again."

After students have thought about the literal "building" in *stru, struct* words like *construction* and *reconstruction*, you can ask them to consider more figurative building. You might, for example, provide these familiar words and ask the students what they have to do with building:

- instruct

- instructor

- instruction

Students will know that these words all deal with teaching: a teacher is an *instructor*, and all students are asked to *follow instructions*. You can guide students in a brief discussion of what school and teaching are all about: Our *instructors* "build" us up by teaching us things we need to know. They build our knowledge. In what ways is a teacher like a builder? A teacher lays a strong foundation for learning—just like a builder who lays a foundation. As we go through school, we advance through grades (*grade* means "step" in Latin) and make our way from first to second to third and so on. Instruction has "steps," just like a building that goes higher and higher. Indeed, when we carefully follow *instructions*, we do step one before step two and so on. With a little discussion, we can get the class to think about the general idea of "building" in figurative terms as well as literal terms.

This activity takes only a few minutes and serves an important purpose: students focus their attention on the new root by connecting to the familiar. You help them do this by scaffolding the conversation through the examples you provide, the tasks you create, and the questions you ask. After the conversations described above, for example, students can independently divide and conquer *stru, struct* words beginning with single-prefix/single-base words like *infrastructure* and then moving to more complex words like *reconstruct* and *indestructible*.

Combine and Create

Knowing that words can be broken down into meaningful units is an important and powerful first step in vocabulary development. Students also need to think about this process from the other direction—to combine word parts to make words. The second routine in the instructional cycle, then, is Combine and Create, in which students complete a variety of activities to compose English words using the root or word part that is the focus of the week's lessons. The point of these activities is for students to work with the selected root in a bit of context. They might be asked to sort words containing the root into categories such as "Words with/without Prefixes." They might be asked to make sentences that contain two or more words with the root of focus. These activities help students identify roots and build connections between roots and the words that contain them.

For example, the Combine and Create lesson for *stru, struct* is a three-column word chart. Students work with partners to decide if given words (e.g., *instruct, instruction, instructor*) are people, things, or actions. Think for a moment about the learning that is embedded in this task: Students consider the "build" aspect of *stru, struct*, to be sure. But they also think and talk about another layer of the relationships among terms—that *instruct, instruction,* and *instructor* have important differences as well as similarities. Research tells us that this focus on similarities and differences is very powerful in promoting learning (Marzano, Pickering, and Pollock 2001).

Read and Reason

Learning how to use the surrounding context, whether grammatical, structural, or oral, helps students expand their vocabularies. Using context clues is an especially important strategy for vocabulary development because, as we noted earlier, many English words have multiple meanings. Identifying which meaning is the best fit depends entirely on context. Moreover, the reason we learn new words is to use them—to understand them in our reading and listening and draw upon them for our writing and speaking. The third routine in the overall instructional cycle, Read and Reason, offers students these opportunities. Students read extended texts—journal entries, advice columns, newspaper accounts, poetry, stories, dialogues, and so forth. These contain several words that feature the root that is the focus of instruction. After reading, students answer questions that depend upon knowledge of both the text they have read and the root they have been learning.

For example, the Read and Reason activity that accompanies the study of *stru*, *struct* is a nonfiction piece about the U.S. highway system. It contains the following *stru*, *struct* words: *construction*, *reconstruct, infrastructure, reconstruction*. After-reading questions ask students about road construction and also how to "divide and conquer" the word *infrastructure*.

Extend and Explore

We want to give students many opportunities to think about and play with the roots we teach. We hope that our instruction will foster an awareness of and interest in words. Open-ended activities that feature student collaboration achieve this goal nicely. The fourth routine in the instructional cycle, Extend and Explore, has two goals. In the short term, we hope to foster additional learning about the root that is the focus of the lesson. In the long term, we want to create lifelong word lovers. Word play (riddles), sketching, and other divergent-thinking activities can contribute to both goals.

The Extend and Explore activity for *stru*, *struct* has two parts, both completed with partners. In the first, students put as many words as possible into a matrix that contains prefixes (e.g., *con-*, *de-*, *in-*) along one dimension and *struct, struction*, and *structive* along the other. Then partners are challenged to make sentences with the words.

Go for the Gold!

The last routine in the instructional cycle is focused on word play. We know that students need multiple opportunities to practice their newfound knowledge of roots. Embedding this practice in game-like activities makes it more palatable, which increases both student persistence and the likelihood that the desired learning will take place. Time for students to play word games—crossword puzzles, word scrambles, word searches, and other enjoyable practice activities—is time well spent.

The Go for the Gold! activity for *stru*, *struct* is a Word Spokes activity. To complete it, students first think of several words containing *stru*, *struct*. Then they write synonyms and antonyms for some of the words. They also define some of the words and use them in sentences.

What's next? You begin again using a new root. You can go through this instructional cycle repeatedly, complete with the five routines, to create a structure for your vocabulary program. But there are two additional issues to consider—how to differentiate instruction and what to do about assessment.

Differentiating Instruction

If you are like most teachers, the range of vocabulary levels among students in your classroom is broad. You want a curriculum that is efficient, yet you also want to offer students instruction and practice that provides the best opportunity for them to learn.

Everyone must be successful. This is particularly important for students who struggle with reading and vocabulary, but it is important for others as well. We all learn more easily when we are effectively engaged—where our motivation, curiosity, and interests are leading the learning. Now think about the opposite—situations that do not lead to successful learning either because the activities are too difficult, because they are too easy, or because a student is struggling with the language. If activities are too difficult or we get tripped up by language barriers, we may become frustrated and think that we'll never get it. If activities are too easy, we become bored because we already know what's being taught. None of these situations leads to the achievement of our long-term goals for students as word learners. We want all students to be successful all the time.

A curiosity-filled environment is one good way to foster this goal. Moreover, in the case of vocabulary learning, we want to entice students to become word lovers for life, which both success and curiosity can foster. Words and language are interesting!

You want to challenge students to grow and support their efforts. Students need a bit of a challenge because this represents room for growth. But too much challenge, or challenge without the assistance they need to succeed, is frustrating. And frustration can lead to feelings of failure. So instruction and practice should challenge students to grow and also offer the support they need to be successful.

With some creativity, many lessons can be adapted for struggling learners, students with advanced knowledge, or English languge learners. The Teacher's Guide for *Building Vocabulary from Word Roots* offers some suggestions for you to consider. The CD that accompanies each level of the series has many additional activities and ideas. Here are a few others, again using the *stru*, *struct* instructional cycle.

For Students Who Struggle

Partners make learning fun, but they also provide extra support for students who need it. When we work alone, it sometimes feels as if we're being tested. Working together with someone else hardly ever feels like this. Partners can serve as recorders, for example, or a partner can just support the struggling learner through quiet conversation.

If students need additional practice to understand the thinking behind Divide and Conquer, give them several easier words featuring the root that is the focus of the instructional cycle. Here are several for *stru, struct: construct, constructed, constructing, instruct, instruction.* You can find these extra words by going to http://onelook.com, entering *struct* (the root with asterisks before and after), and selecting the "Common words only" search. You'll get more words than you need, but skimming the list is easy.

Students can keep vocabulary journals. They could devote a couple of pages to each root, perhaps including its meaning and several key words containing it. It may help to break some of these words apart, as in Divide and Conquer: indestructible = *in* (not) + *de* (apart) + *struct* (build) + *ible* = "cannot be taken apart." When students find *stru, struct* words in their reading, they can add them to the appropriate journal page.

For Advanced Students

The resource http://onelook.com comes in handy for advanced students as well. The "Common words only" search on *struct* yields 94 words. What could students do with these? They could select some words and make crossword puzzles or word searches (see Appendices A and B for online resources for this). They could make riddles for others to solve. They could look for opposites (e.g., *structured-unstructured; superstructure-substructure*). They could sort words by syllables or in some other way. With imagination, you and your advanced students will find numerous ways to use many of these words.

Students can use online resources (see Appendix A) to learn more about words of interest. From the *struct* search, you might want to ask them to find out about *obstructionists* or *constructivism*, for example. Or you might simply ask students to select a couple of words that they find interesting and find out more about them.

For English Language Learners

English language learners (ELL) need to focus on meaning, using research-based strategies to try out new words. They need frequent opportunities to try out new words in varied learning contexts. Adding context to the language is one of the most important keys to success with English learners. Provide sentences to go with the words you are teaching for the lesson. Try to reduce the number of words or word roots, too, since ELL students will need more time to work through the activities. It is also a good idea to read the sentences or words aloud. Hearing the words will increase their verbal interaction and they can relate the sounds to the written words.

ELL students generally need more distinctive and frequent support. Preteach lessons with ELL students so they understand the meaning of the word roots. Then, class discussion will support further comprehension and word leaning. For a more in-depth discussion of English language learners, see pages 22–24 in Chapter 1.

Differentiating instruction is important, but doing so doesn't mean that different groups of students need to work with different roots. The adaptations provided on pp. 47–49 can easily be integrated into the overall instructional cycle so that the classroom community can share some instructional time. Yet, with these adaptations, everyone is challenged, everyone is supported, and, most importantly, everyone is successful.

Vocabulary Assessment

One aspect of an effective vocabulary program is the assessment that accompanies it. We want to know that students' active and passive vocabularies are growing. Unfortunately, this is a difficult task. According to Pearson et al., "Our measures of vocabulary are inadequate to the challenge of documenting the relationship between word learning and global measures of comprehension" (2007, 283).

Until the research community develops accurate vocabulary assessments, we need to use informal assessment measures. Each level of *Building Vocabulary from Word Roots* contains a vocabulary pre-test and post-test that focus on some roots addressed at that level. Using the pre-test will help you determine how to differentiate instruction: who needs to be challenged, for example, as well as who needs extra support. Using the post-test will provide some information on the extent to which students have learned the new roots.

You may be interested in more general vocabulary assessment. Here are some additional assessment ideas to try. Keep in mind that none of these offers a complete picture of students' word learning, but each adds information that allows you to see the picture more completely.

1. When you confer with students and listen to them read, select several words from the text selection. Ask students to define the words or use them in sentences that show their meaning. Judge student success with a three-point rubric: Outstanding, Satisfactory, Unsatisfactory. Unsatisfactory responses are either clearly wrong or absent, as in a student indicating that he or she doesn't know what a word means. The difference between "satisfactory" and "outstanding" is a matter of degree—outstanding responses tend to be more elaborate or offer extended examples. You can keep track of students' performance anecdotally or by using a simple two-column chart with the titles "Word" and "Rating." You can even return to words initially rated "satisfactory" or "unsatisfactory" at a later time to see if student knowledge of the words in question has deepened.

2. Ask students to make lists of special words from their unaided writing. Look at these lists and evaluate the sophistication of the words using the O-S-U scale described above.

3. Use Knowledge Rating Charts. Select key words from a text students will read. Make a three-column chart for students to indicate if they know a word well, have seen or heard it,

or don't know it at all. Blachowicz and Fisher note that this activity helps students come to understand "that knowing the meaning of a word is not something that happens all at once" (2006, 100). Of course, perusing students' responses can provide you with good assessment information as well. Here is a sample chart using a few words from this paragraph:

Word	Know it well	Have heard it or seen it	Don't know it at all
knowledge			
activity			
understand			

Using a student's chart for assessment purposes means that you trust the student has answered thoughtfully. Nonetheless, what could you learn if a student marked that he or she knew all these words well? What could you do to check quickly on the student's perceptions of his or her word knowledge?

4. Encourage self assessment. Students can and should have some say in evaluating their own vocabulary growth. In addition to fostering students' sense of responsibility for their own learning, self-assessment is often motivating. Moreover, self-assessment sends a subtle reminder about the importance of words and word learning. Each time they assess themselves, students will think about vocabulary as an abstract concept. Over time, they will think about "word awareness" as they read. You might want to ask students to write about their own word knowledge in their journals, for example. You might want them to write definitions of new concepts in their own words, or reflect more broadly on the new words they have learned or on the value of word learning. Ask them to describe where they find new and

interesting words. Ask them to identify which strategies they use most often to figure out the meaning of new words (Newton, Padak, and Rasinski 2008).

We hope you have found this chapter *instructive* with regard to the *instructional* basics. Moreover, we hope your *instruction* will be full of success and full of fun for your students and for you, the *instructor*.

Chapter 4

Getting into Words: A Developmental Look at Vocabulary Instruction

Lucas jumped into bed, eager for his dad to read him a bedtime story. It was one of his favorite times of the day. "We're learning all sorts of stuff about words in school," Lucas said as he got comfortable in his bed. Dad asked about what kinds of "stuff" he was learning, and Lucas told him about compound words. "Well, are you ready for your bedtime story?" Dad asked. Lucas replied with excitement, "Yep!" Dad showed Lucas the cover of a book of poems, including the picture and the title. "This book is called *Where the Sidewalk Ends*, by Shel Silverstein," Dad said. Then they read the title together, pausing briefly after each word, when suddenly Lucas shouted, "Hey, *sidewalk* is a compound word, isn't it?"

Mr. Johnson, Lucas's first-grade teacher, had begun to teach students about the roots we have described thus far in this book. He began with the idea of compound words, since this is an easy way to help students understand that words can have meaning chunks as well as sound chunks. He used the instructional basics that we outlined in the last chapter, both the general principles to guide instruction and the routines that can constitute an effective vocabulary program. But he also thought about his students' developmental needs.

This chapter is about designing instruction that meets students' developmental needs. First, we focus on how to get students "into words." That is, how do we teach students how and why to look for meaning inside of words? How do we help students who are new to the classroom or new to the idea of word roots?

Compound Words

As we mentioned in Chapter 2, we want primary students to begin to think about roots (meaning units), as well as phonemes (sound units). If this process begins with familiar words, students will develop this new learning in the context of the known. In other words, we can get students into words by asking them to focus on these familiar words and examine them for parts that have meaning (their roots). The description below outlines procedures that have proven useful.

Begin with two-syllable compound words that students already know. That is, students should know each word that makes the compound, as well as the compound itself. Here are some examples:

- bedroom
- birthday
- football
- snowflake
- playground
- classroom
- sidewalk

To introduce the idea of compounds, you might print a sentence on the board or on chart paper:

- I painted my *bedroom* blue and white.

Then you can read the sentence to students while pointing at the words. Repeat a couple of times, if necessary, until you know that students know the words. At this point, you can draw students' attention to the compound word. Try posing a riddle: "What do you call the *room* where your *bed* is?" When students reply, "bedroom," point to it in the sentence and show students how *bedroom* is made up of *bed* and *room*. Try this a few more times:

- Tomorrow is my *birthday*. What do you call the *day* of your *birth*?

- Do you like to play *football*? What do you call a *ball* you kick with your *foot*?

To conclude the lesson, tell students that *bedroom, birthday,* and *football* are called compound words, and that compound words are made up of two words that together tell the meaning of the compound.

The next day, return to the examples. This time, simply read the sentences and ask students to identify the compound word in each. As they do, remind them that compound words are made up of two words. Challenge students to identify the words. You might want to show the additive nature of compounds like this:

- bed + room = bedroom

- birth + day = birthday

- foot + ball = football

You could also separate the words with a slash mark:

- bed/room

- birth/day

- foot/ball

You may then want to offer more compounds. Ask students to divide each word into its two "meaningful" parts. Then have them talk about each word using phrases or sentences that include each of its units. They may offer such statements as, "A sidewalk is something you walk on alongside the road"; "A snowflake is a flake of snow"; "Our school has grounds we can play on." The point is not to get technical about definitions. The purpose of the lesson is to get students thinking about how semantic units are connected to produce meaning.

After students understand the concept of compound words, you might invite them to be on the lookout for other compound words. These words can be listed on a "Compound Words" word wall. Around the school, students might notice *hallway, desktop, chalkboard, notebook, backpack, laptop,* etc. If students offer suggestions that the dictionary lists as two separate words (rather than as a compound word), accept their suggestions without belaboring the point that some words are written as two words. For example, students might suggest a term like *school clothes*. Remember, the overall goals are to build understanding about compound words and, more importantly, to build concepts about meaning within word parts.

After students understand bisyllabic compound words, you can show them words that are three or four syllables long. Repeat the process just outlined, asking students to divide these slightly longer but still easily recognizable words into their component parts. Some examples might be:

- Spiderman
- schoolteacher
- storybook
- dishwasher
- mountaintop
- countertop
- hairdresser

In order to generate words, you can ask students to think about parts of their houses, various occupations, or favorite activities. They might come up with words like *waterfall, loudspeaker, watercolors, scorekeeper, honeybee,* etc. Add these words to the word wall. Ask students to talk about each word using its component parts: "Spiderman is a *man* who moves like/looks like a *spider*"; "A storybook is a *book* with *stories* in it"; "A dishwasher is a person or a machine that *washes dishes*," and so on. By discussing easy, everyday words that are three syllables or longer, students begin to see that there is nothing intimidating about long words if we know how to "divide and conquer" them. The important thing at this early stage is to empower students to look inside words to find meaning, not just sounds.

Negating Words with Prefixes

The next step teaches students to identify words that begin with negative prefixes (e.g., *un-* and *in-*). We ask them to mark off the negative prefix, separating it from the rest of the word using a slash (e.g., un/wrap) or using an equation (e.g., un + wrap = unwrap). Then they identify the rest of the word. Again we invite them to talk about the word, this time using "no" or "not" in their descriptions. We start with words containing *un-* that present recognizable words when detached from the prefix. Examples include:

- unwrap
- unbutton
- unzip
- unhappy
- unable
- unhealthy
- unclear

As students talk about these negated words, they may say, "After I *un*wrap my presents, they are *no* longer wrapped"; "My shirt is *not* buttoned if it is *un*buttoned"; "When my jacket is *un*zipped, it is *not* zipped," and so on. This is an easy exercise, but it teaches an important skill: students are learning to translate a prefix into its meaning and combine the meaning of the prefix with the rest of the word.

We can then advance to the negative prefix *in-*, which means "not." We present such words as:

- incorrect
- incomplete
- inaccurate
- indefinite
- inhuman
- invisible

The words are getting longer, but they can be divided, and their meanings can be deduced by working with the prefix. After students detach the negative prefix from such words, they find that the rest of each word is fully recognizable. They simply translate these words as meaning "not correct," "not complete," "not accurate," and so on.

If necessary, make riddles to support students' understanding: "What do we call something that is *not* visible?" Eventually, most students will see how to translate prefixes. Furthermore, they are getting used to the idea of dividing and conquering—and looking for meaning as they do so. In some cases, the divided units are recognizable as intact words (e.g., *bedroom, incorrect*). In other cases, part of the word requires translation (e.g., the *un-* prefix in *unbutton*).

Some Directional Prefixes

Two prefixes in particular lend themselves very well to instruction for primary-level students: the directional prefixes *pre-* ("before") and *re-* ("back, again"). We follow the same procedure recommended for compound words and *in-/un-*. Present students with simple sentences that contain words beginning with these prefixes. After reading the sentences with students and identifying the target words, ask students to detach the prefix. When they do this, an intact, recognizable word remains. Here are some sample *pre-* words from everyday phrases:

- presoak laundry
- prewashed lettuce
- preheat an oven
- pregame show
- preshrunk jeans

After students remove the prefix, they are left with a word they already know and may recognize on sight. Ask them to talk about these words using the "before" meaning of the prefix *pre-* in their comments: We *pre*soak heavily stained clothes "before" we wash them with other clothes; We *pre*heat the oven "before" we put the cookie sheets in; *Pre*washed lettuce has been washed "before" we buy it at the store, and so on.

Do the same thing with the prefix *re-*. Again, use words that are recognizable after the prefix is detached. Ask students to talk about these words using "back" or "again" in their comments. For example:

- rewrite
- redo
- refills
- rebuild
- reruns

Students may offer such comments as: *re*write: Go "back" and write this "again"; *re*do: I want you to do your homework "again," go "back" and *re*do it; *re*fills: They give free *re*fills at that restaurant—they let you fill your glass "again," and you can go "back" as many times as you want, and so on.

This instruction may span several weeks. Take time to show students how words are made up of parts that have meaning. Give them ample time to practice in a lighthearted, fun way. Although the Divide and Conquer routine is presented with simple, familiar words, the concept itself is critical to further word learning. Students will be learning a strategy that they can apply to new words throughout their years in school and beyond.

Word Composition

So far, instruction has focused on recognizing words and word parts. We have presented compound words and words with prefixes and asked students to identify what they see. This helps students develop control over their passive vocabularies—the words they encounter when reading. Building active vocabulary is important, too. A good way to approach this is to use riddles. For example, you might ask, "What do you do when you read a sentence 'again'?" They will answer, "We *reread* it." "When your parents tell you to make your bed 'again,' what do you do?" Answer, "We *remake* it." Answering these questions gives students practice in learning how to generate active vocabulary by producing the word that fits the context. This process, word composition, represents an important next step in students' word learning.

You might also ask students to make up silly words using the prefixes they have learned. Most students find it fun to generate their own vocabulary. They can work with partners to make their own riddles that describe a thing or activity: "I am thinking of a word. What word is it?" Then they can ask their classmates to produce the word they have in mind. They might make up words and have some fun playing with them. Some examples might include:

- I wish I had "not drunk" all that milk. I wish I could *undrink* it.

- I wish I had "not read" that story. If only I could *unread* it.

- I spent all my money "before" I went shopping. I *prespent* my money.

- My mom drove me "back" to school after I had forgotten my books. She *redrove* me.

What Are Students Learning?

Before we consider what is going on during these activities, we should ask, "What is *not* going on?" Students are not learning word lists. They are not actively memorizing columns of individual words that have no relationship to one another. This surface approach to word learning is not effective; students quickly forget words learned from memorized word lists. Nor is it efficient because, as we noted in Chapter 1, research shows that students can learn only 8–10 new words per week through direct instruction.

For all their simplicity, the lessons we have described thus far in this chapter teach students several things at once. As they gain facility with the Divide and Conquer strategy, students find themselves thinking about roots, which appear over and over again not only in school words but also in their everyday speech. At the primary level, these word parts are often intact words themselves (e.g., *bedroom* and *snowflake*). Even so, students can begin translating some of these units (in words like *unbutton*, *preheat*, and *rewrite*). They are learning to read the prefix *un-* as meaning "not," the prefix *pre-* as "before," and the prefix *re-* as "back, again." In the process, they are applying these small semantic units over and over again to different bases, both in terms of taking words apart and putting words together. When they learn how to divide and conquer, they also learn how to combine and create. Rather than memorizing word lists, the roots approach emphasizes learning the prefixes, bases, and suffixes that occur with the greatest frequency in the English language. Since there's nothing conceptually difficult about such words as *before*, *not*, and *again*, students can learn more than one root per week. Each root generates potentially dozens of words.

A well-known adage comes to mind here: "Give a man a fish and you feed him for a day; teach a man to fish and you feed him for a lifetime." We can apply this saying to the learning and teaching of vocabulary: "If we give students word lists, they may have vocabulary for the day. But if we teach them how to divide and conquer, they will have vocabulary for life."

Some Easy Suffixes

Once students have grown accustomed to looking for a prefix at the beginning of a word, they will be prepared to do the same thing with suffixes. By having students look at the beginning and end of a word, they learn to search for word parts that have meaning: the word's beginning, middle, and end. As we draw their attention to suffixes, we again present them with everyday words, taking examples from what they already know. We teach them a few suffixes that have fixed meanings. Our goal is not to teach them all the suffixes, only to draw their attention to them and teach students how to work with suffixes. Some useful and easy suffixes for this level are:

- *-er* = "more"

- *-est* = "most"

- *-ful* = "full of"

- *-less* = "without, lacking"

- *-able*, *-ible* = "can, able to"

We can present the first two suffixes in a single lesson and sequence such adjectives as *small, smaller, smallest; tall, taller, tallest; smart, smarter, smartest*, etc. The base of each of these words is already known: *small, tall, smart*. We explain that when we add the suffixes *-er* and *-est* to words like these, we change the meaning of the base word. (These are adjectives, but it is not necessary to get into the technicalities of parts of speech at this stage.) Students can be asked to draw pictures of three things of varying sizes. One student may draw three dogs: one is small, another is "more small," and the third is the "most small." They may caption each drawing with "small dog," "smaller dog," "smallest dog." Another may draw three houses, three people, and so on. A next step might also involve drawings: students can share their drawings without labels and ask partners, "Which is the smallest house?" "Which is the smaller of these two houses?" and so forth.

By looking at these suffixes as units with meaning, students quickly learn that they can change the meaning of a word by adding a suffix to a base word, by removing a suffix, or by changing the suffix. In the process, they learn that since a word is made of parts that have meaning, they can figure out the meanings of words by looking for parts. These parts appear over and over again in words that they encounter every day.

Likewise, we can teach the two suffixes *-ful* and *-less* as a set and have the students generate antonyms. Here are some pairs to work with:

• careful	• careless
• colorful	• colorless
• harmful	• harmless
• hopeful	• hopeless
• meaningful	• meaningless
• painful	• painless

- powerful
- powerless
- thoughtful
- thoughtless
- useful
- useless

You might begin by showing students two pictures—one in color and the other in black and white. Ask, "Which one is *colorful*?" and "Which one is *colorless*?" You could also show *careful* and *careless* children, *harmful* and *harmless* gadgets, and so on. Then you might ask students to make quick sketches: "Sketch something *useful*," "Sketch something *useless*," and so on. Finally, students can draw pairs of pictures independently and caption them with words of opposite meaning: a *careful* student as opposed to a *careless* student, a *colorful* sunset as opposed to a *colorless* day, and so on. All of these activities will help students learn that the same base can produce words of opposite meaning depending on the suffix they attach. This insight reinforces students' understanding that the meaning of a word is significantly affected by the parts it contains. Students are making the cognitive leap that words contain much more than letters and sounds; many are also made up of semantic units—roots. Just as the roots of a tree are essential to the tree's life, the roots of a word are essential to the word's meaning. We may not have noticed roots before, but dividing and conquering a word makes them visible. Word awareness is beginning! Students are uncovering what is inside a word as they dig for its roots.

We can invite students to engage in word play. They can create their own words by using a single suffix. The suffix *-able* lends itself well to this exercise. As students attach this suffix to any number of existing words, they talk about the meaning they have generated. Examples:

- A *readable* book: it "can" be read.
- A *doable* assignment: it "can" be done.
- A *washable* jacket: it "can" be washed.
- An *unthinkable* idea: it "can not" be thought.

Just as we invited students to engage in word composition with prefixes, we can also encourage them to use suffixes to make up words they have never heard or seen before. They can talk about the new ideas they are presenting as they create their own vocabulary. Some fun vocabulary might include:

- My dog is *unwalkable* because he refuses to wear a collar and leash: he "can not" be walked.

- My jacket is *unzippable* because it only has buttons: it "can not" be zipped.

- My bed is *unsleepable* because the mattress is so lumpy: it "can not" be slept in.

By encouraging our students to create their own vocabulary from word parts, we embolden them to think as they speak and write. They learn that word mastery involves two skills. As lifelong readers and listeners of words, they will always be encountering vocabulary they can "divide and conquer." Furthermore, as lifelong speakers and writers, they will benefit from combining and creating roots as they come up with the right word for the right context. But perhaps most importantly, when we ask students to generate vocabulary by using suffixes and prefixes, we are preparing them for the most important part of the Divide and Conquer strategy: zeroing in on the base.

Back to "Basics"

Most likely, when you are helping students learn to focus on prefixes and suffixes, they will notice that prefixes and suffixes are always attached to something else in the word. That "something else" is the base. Of the three kinds of roots (prefix, base, suffix), the base is the most important. Indeed, the base is the crucial part of the word: it provides the word with its essential, core, or "basic" meaning. That meaning is affected by the prefix and by the suffix. By themselves, the prefix and suffix cannot generate a word. There must be a base.

Fortunately, the meanings of bases derived from Latin and Greek are usually simple and straightforward. Our sample base in Chapter 2 was *mot* = "move." Here are two more Latin bases and their meanings:

- *audi, audit* = "hear, listen"
- *vid, vis*   = "see"

The meaning of many words built on such bases is often immediately clear. An *audible* sound, for example, is one that "can" be "heard." A *visible* image "can" be "seen." An *inaudible* voice "can not" be "heard," just as an *invisible* force "can not" be "seen." An *auditorium* is a large room for "listening" to speakers or performers. This is why auditoriums are designed for acoustics (*acous* is the Greek base for "hear"). The *audio* portion of a TV program is the part we "hear" (as opposed to the *video* portion, which we "see"). We only "listen" to an *audiotape*, while we can "see" the images on a *videotape*. When we *audition* for a school play, we must speak a part, sing a song, or play an instrument for the judges to "hear" or "listen" to. A *vista* offers a panoramic "view" and enables us to "see" large expanses of scenery. We wear a sun *visor* to shade our eyes so that we can "see" things in the glaring sunlight. In words such as these, the straightforward meaning of the base leads directly to the meaning of the entire word. Students will quickly find the basic idea of "hearing" or "seeing" as readily *evident* in these words (*e-* = intensifying prefix; things that are evident are "very" easy to "see").

"Metaphors Be with You": Helping Students with Figurative Meaning

But how are we to help students understand that these words are also derived from *vid, vis: advise, supervise, provide,* and *provisions*? The basic and literal meaning of "see" isn't readily evident in these words. But if you begin exploration of *vid, vis* with words related to actual physical "seeing," you can scaffold students' learning about this other, more abstract "seeing." To do this, you can return to the overall procedure we described earlier—ask the students to talk about (i.e., not define) the words and figure out how they contain the basic idea of seeing on perhaps a different level from that of physical eyesight.

Let us consider the word *supervisor* and talk about it in terms of seeing (prefix *super-* = "over"). A supervisor is someone who "oversees" someone else's work. Ask students to talk about supervisors and what they do. We may speak of our supervisor at work as hovering over us and watching our every move. The basic meaning of "seeing" forms the core of this word. A supervisor takes a close "look" at our work and inspects it for accuracy. We might ask, for example, "What does a *supervisor* do? What could this have to do with 'seeing'?" As students offer ideas, rephrase their answers to focus on the words *seeing, watching,* or *looking.* This will help students begin to think about seeing both literally and figuratively.

We can find the same basic idea of "seeing" in the words *provide* and *provisions.* We use these words in such contexts as "providing for our children," "providing for a rainy day," "buying weekly provisions at the grocery store," and so on. When we shop for our *provisions*, we are "seeing ahead" (*pro-* = "forward, ahead") to what we will need for the coming week. When we *provide* for our children, we are "seeing ahead" to their future needs. We are *envisioning* the future, trying to form a mental picture of what they will need. The basic sense of "seeing" in all these words is not literal, but figurative.

But how are we to teach the concept of figurative uses of language in vocabulary lessons? Isn't this something we find in poetry and other high forms of literature? Actually, figurative language abounds in our daily speaking. We use the word *see* on a literal and figurative level, and we use these two levels without even thinking about the difference. As linguists George Lakoff and Mark Johnson (1980) have demonstrated, figurative language, especially metaphors, guide our very thought processes. They are embedded in our vocabulary. As we discuss the word *supervisor*, we can invite students to recall phrases from our daily speech when we might say "see" without referring to physical eyesight. We might say, "Don't you see my point?" In this context, "see" refers to understanding, to seeing something with the mind's eye, as it were. This meaning of "see" in "Don't you see?" is different from saying something like, "Don't you see that bus?" When we "see" a bus, we literally see it with our eyes. When we "see" someone's point, we take the basic meaning of "see" and apply it to other contexts—even with our eyes closed! When something is *evident*, we say, "Oh, now I see!"

You can help students see the differences between these two kinds of "seeing" by presenting several phrases or sentences containing *see*. For example:

- Do you see my point?
- Do you see the rainbow?
- See to it...
- See the pretty picture.
- Now I see what you mean.
- Now I see a storm cloud.

Ask students to work with partners to sort these into two categories: physical seeing and figurative seeing, or "seeing with our eyes" and "seeing in our mind's eye." When they share their work with the rest of the group, be sure to invite their thinking about which kind of seeing is being referred to in the phrase or sentence. You could even post two charts in the classroom and ask students to add examples they encounter.

On the one hand, understanding the meaning of bases on a figurative level poses a challenge to teachers and students. On the other hand, these bases provide a fascinating entrance into the world of conceptual thinking. Our everyday speech is filled with figurative language. It abounds in colloquial English, and these colloquialisms can often lead us to an understanding of words' meanings.

Learning to think about words' figurative meanings can help students with another common problem. In the first chapter, we mentioned that a word like *revolution* means one thing in science class (e.g., the revolution of Earth around the sun) and another thing in history class (e.g., the American Revolution). This polysemy can pose problems for students, but knowing roots and knowing how to think figuratively about meaning can lead to solutions. We can advise students to examine the context of a polysemous word to figure out what it means "this time." Guiding students to contextual clues remains an important part of vocabulary instruction, but the roots approach offers additional support. If a student knows that the base of the word *revolution* is *volut*, meaning "roll, turn," he or she can work with the base meaning and arrive at a correct understanding of the word in each context. In science class, we speak literally of Earth "rolling, turning" around the sun as it physically moves through space. But in history, we speak of revolution figuratively, in terms of the first Americans "overturning" the British rule of the colonies. Revolutions upset things because they turn political situations upside down. The basic idea of "rolling, turning" lies at the core of the word *revolution* whether we are speaking of the American Revolution or the revolution of the moon around Earth. To drive the meaning of the base home, we might tell students that the first books (which we now call *volumes*) were made of "rolls" of ancient paper called papyrus!

"Run" with This

Let's think about the literal and figurative meanings of bases with another example. The Latin bases *cur(r)*, *curs*, and *cour(s)* mean "run." In many words, this base refers to physical "running," or something close to it: a *courier* service "runs" letters and packages with runners who either run on foot, ride bikes, or drive delivery trucks. The idea of "running, speed, rapid movement" is evident in this word. We may also think of a *racecourse* on which athletes, cars, or horses physically "run." In the poem, "'Twas the Night Before Christmas," we read, "Onward his coursers they came!" Santa's reindeer are fast runners.

What about writing in *cursive* script? There is no physical running in writing cursive. In fact, we usually write in cursive while we are sitting down! In this word, the "running" occurs on a figurative level. When we write in cursive, our letters "run" together with ligatures, and we can write more quickly than when we merely print in block letters. As we think about figurative running, we observe that the *cursor* on our computer screen "runs" across the monitor screen as we move our mouse. The *current* of a river has "running water." Reflect on this phrase for a moment. If we thought in merely literal terms, the phrase "running water" would strike us as absurd. Water does not run—it flows; it spills; it drips. But it does not literally run. It figuratively runs. The figurative meaning also pertains when we speak of *current* events, of films *currently* showing at the theater. These events and films are now "running," as we say. We employ figurative language in our daily speech, and this can lead us to a roots-level understanding of many words.

Here are a few more "running" words that employ figurative language. We speak of cash as *currency* because we look on money as flowing, fleeting, running—similar to the current of water. Compare phrases like "cash flow," "liquidated assets," and "frozen assets." We *incur* debts and "run up" our bills. When we *concur* with others on an issue, we agree with them because we go or "run together with" them. When we take an *excursion*, we are usually riding "out," not "running out." Nevertheless, the basic figurative use of "running" applies. Likewise, one country may conduct a military *incursion* of another, an aggressive "running into" someone else's territory. The invading soldiers may arrive in tanks or by parachute without actually running on foot. In a relatively new application of the word *incursion*, we hear of *runway incursions* at airports with heavy traffic. Airplanes have near misses and almost "run" "into" one another as they land and take off.

A Coherent Pedagogy

As we focus on word roots with their literal and figurative meanings, it is important to get our students talking about their school vocabulary in everyday speech. This is important for several reasons. First, we are removing the fear factor from vocabulary. Dictionary definitions can be intimidating for students. They often look up a new word only to find that the definition is just as hard to decipher as the word itself. Formal definitions that include such phrases as *characterized by*, *pertaining to*, *having a tendency to*, do not have a particularly inviting tone that will encourage the student to keep reading. Little wonder that many students do not like to open a dictionary! If students think that they have to sound like a dictionary in order to prove mastery of the word, they can quickly become discouraged and give up, saying, "I can never talk like this. Nobody talks like this!"

Second, students learn that by talking about a word in terms of its roots, they often have background knowledge they can activate. They simply may not have realized that they had this foundation already at their disposal. Students may never have heard a word like *incursion* before, but they all know what *run* means. By approaching vocabulary on this literally "basic" level, students learn to simplify something that they initially find complex. *Incursion* is a difficult word when first encountered, but the concepts of an army "running into" enemy territory (*military incursion*) or of one airplane "running into" another (*runway incursion*) are understandable at once.

Third, as students focus on the roots they recognize inside a new word, they can become inspired to recall words they already know but perhaps never thought about as cognates. Students thus learn that words have their own families, and that words with the same base all share a basic meaning. A student who first encounters a word like *incursion* and identifies the base as meaning "run," may well associate it with words he or she either uses or hears all the time—words like *current*, *currency*, *course*, *cursor*, *excursion*, and so on. These moments of discovery when a student sees a connection between a new word and one or more cognates can be exciting. The student is not only learning a new word but also recalling knowledge already acquired. The student feels gratified and rewarded for knowing something.

Finally, the roots approach to vocabulary learning and teaching is important because it mirrors the very process through which we, as users of language, arrive at an understanding of new ideas and concepts. Let's take the example of the *automobile*. We all know what automobiles are, of course, but this was not always the case. When the automobile was first invented, we had no word to describe this strange machine on wheels that was able to move itself without an animal to pull it. So we gave it a name from two roots: the Greek *auto-* meaning "self" and the Latin *mobil* meaning "move." The Greek and Latin roots in the newly contrived word gave us a handle for understanding the novel invention. But this contraption was so novel that we could not fully understand it without likening it to something we already knew. We could only understand the automobile by activating our background knowledge. So we turned to the horse and buggy, the only device that offered something comparable; this was our figure or metaphor for conceiving of this contraption. We thus arrived at a clear understanding of the automobile through metaphorical or figurative thinking. We still see signs of this pattern of thought in such phrases as the "horsepower" of an engine; the "power train" (think of "wagon train"); and the very words "car" (from the original "horseless carriage"), "drive" (originally, to get a horse moving), and "ride" (we ride a horse). We speak of cars "breaking down," a phrase first applied to horses whose strength gave out, and of riding "shotgun" in the front seat (originally, the position for the gunman on a horse-drawn wagon, beside the driver). Among the nicknames given to the first cars by their owners, we find such "equine" terms as "Tin Lizzie" (Lizzie being the pet name for a mare) and "Ole Bess." To this day, automobile marketers invoke our figurative thinking with such names for their products as Bronco, Mustang, Pinto, Colt, etc.

The point here is simple but very important: as thinkers and users of language, we all come to understand new things only in terms of what we already know. This is how learning and its associated vocabulary advance. We activate our own background knowledge by likening the new concept or invention to something familiar. In the process, we approach the new idea on a "basic" level, which we then apply both literally (e.g., a *courier* physically "runs" to deliver packages) and figuratively (the *cursor* figuratively "runs" across my computer screen). The roots approach to vocabulary mirrors this very process. Thus, as we teach our students to "get into words" at the root level, we actually invoke the same thought processes all users of language invoke when they advance from the known to the unknown. This pedagogy is in line with the very evolution of our language and our own development as language speakers.

Summary

In this chapter, we described a developmental sequence for teaching students about units of meaning in the words they encounter. This sequence begins with compound words because they are concrete, familiar, and useful for making the "meaning" point. If you are beginning this roots approach to word learning at the primary level, we recommend that you spend a few weeks on compounds. If you are working with older students who have not previously studied word roots, you may need only a day or two. The common prefixes and suffixes we present in this chapter are also an appropriate instructional emphasis for young children. You may need less instructional time with older students who are beginning roots study. The time you spend— whether several weeks or a few days—is important, for it helps students understand the core of this approach: many words are made up of meaning units.

The figurative meanings of common bases may be most appropriate for intermediate or middle-grade students. But once they become accustomed to this way of thinking about words, you will be amazed at how easily they embrace it. Asking what the

American Revolution has to do with "turn," for example, poses an interesting problem for students. It invites critical thinking about the word and also the concepts represented by the word.

In *Building Vocabulary from Word Roots*, we provide rich and ample discussions of the literal and figurative meanings of all the bases presented. We also offer many more examples of compounds (Level 3), as well as prefixes and suffixes (all levels). Roots-based vocabulary instruction turns even young children like Lucas, who was mentioned at the beginning of this chapter, into word sleuths.

#50472—Greek and Latin Roots

Chapter 5

Vocabulary Practice Activities

Practice makes perfect. We've all heard it. Practice helps us learn new skills like playing tennis or golf, and driving a car or boat. Practice allows us to become comfortable with a complex activity and to participate in it without thinking about its individual parts. We learn how to coordinate and integrate the parts of the skill into the whole.

What makes a good practice activity? Consider the example of learning to drive a car. One important criterion is difficulty level—we would not ask a new driver to negotiate an expressway during rush hour. Another criterion is support (or scaffolding)—parents or driving instructors often ride along with novice drivers. And probably the most important criterion is authenticity—someone who wants to learn to drive must eventually "hit the streets." These three criteria—difficulty level, support or scaffolding, and authenticity—apply to practice in reading and learning new vocabulary, as well as all the other practice we provide in school.

In reading, we give students time each day to practice by reading independently. This helps them learn to orchestrate the parts of reading—decoding, fluency, and comprehension—into a meaningful and engaging activity. We help students find books that may be a little challenging but will not frustrate them. Teachers often scaffold independent reading by beginning with small amounts of time and gradually increasing independent reading time. And certainly, independent reading is an authentic form of practicing the skills of reading—more authentic than completing activity sheets, for example.

What characterizes a good practice activity for vocabulary learning? The criterion of difficulty level, applied to vocabulary practice, may suggest the need to differentiate. Students may complete the same activity but with different words or word parts. After all, in a class of 25 students, it doesn't make much sense to assume that everyone needs to practice the same things. Think about your English language learners, advanced students, and struggling students. What accommodations can you make for them? Support or scaffolding in vocabulary practice can come from the teacher while leading or modeling activities. Support can also come from peers. When partners work through an activity together, they often teach each other. Moreover, the very process of talking through activities supports learning. The criterion of authenticity applies to vocabulary practice too. And here, keeping instructional principles in mind is helpful. Three of the guidelines for vocabulary instruction that we presented earlier in this book also apply to vocabulary practice:

- Students need strategies for determining word meaning that will help them become metacognitively and metalinguistically aware (Nagy and Scott 2000).

- Students should be immersed in words, with frequent opportunities to use new words in diverse oral and print contexts in order to learn them on a deep level (Blachowicz and Fisher 2002, 2006).

- Vocabulary instruction must foster word consciousness, an awareness of and interest in words (Graves and Watts-Taffe 2002).

The practice activities that follow are based on these principles. We have used these activities successfully in our own work with students, and we know dozens of other teachers who have done likewise. The format for each description is similar: purpose, materials, general procedures, and adaptations for different situations or groups of learners. Where possible, we have also included citations so that you can read more about these activities if you wish.

Word Spokes

(Rasinski et al. 2006)

This activity is designed to develop students' word analysis skills. It can be done individually, in a small group, or in partners. Necessary materials include a Word Spokes template (see below) and roots or word parts for students to work with. Either you or the students may select these roots.

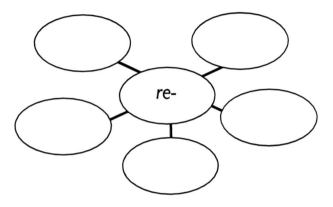

General Procedures:

1. If the activity is new for students, you may want to begin by reviewing the concept that some words have root parts that provide clues to word meaning. Use a familiar example such as *re-*, and remind students that *re-* always means "back" or "again," as in *reheat, review,* or *rerun.* Invite students to explain what *re-* means in each example by using the words "back" or "again" (e.g., *reheat* means "heat again").

2. Put a blank Word Spokes template on an overhead transparency, a large piece of chart paper, or the board. Write the prefix *re-* (or the word part you used in the introduction described in step 1) in the center circle, and invite students to "spoke" out five different words that have the prefix *re-*. If students need extra support, you can use one of the example words from step 1 (e.g., *reheat*).

3. As students call out words, write them on separate spokes. Ask students to describe the definitional aspects of the word parts (e.g., the "back" or "again" aspect of the *re-* words). You might even want to write the word like an equation: *re*heat = *re* + heat = heat "again."

These three steps are necessary only if the activity is new to students or if they need a reminder at the beginning of a new school year. After students learn the activity, you may want to duplicate several blank Word Spokes templates so that they can select this as an independent activity.

Adaptations:

1. Students might select word parts independently, from a list of review words, or from new words being introduced.

2. Ask students to write the "equations" for the words they use.

3. Ask students to write sentences that show the words' meanings.

4. Partners or peer tutors can act as scribes for younger students or struggling readers. In such cases, be sure that the partner knows how to ask questions rather than provide words for the student.

5. Even if everyone is doing a Word Spokes activity, you can vary the difficulty level by asking students to use different word parts. You can also provide hints to add extra support (e.g., on the Word Spoke for *re*heat, you could add "this means 'heat again'" or "you might do this with leftovers").

6. When students have worked on the same root, point out the variety of words that contain the root and the different ways in which the root can be used. When students have worked on different roots, ask questions about why they chose their words. Talking about the words is a good way to have students practice using them.

7. Follow the Word Spokes activity with a series of directions that invite students to choose and use all the words they have generated in different ways. Here are some of our favorite follow-up directions:

   a. Pick one of the words and write two synonyms.

   b. Pick one of the words and write two antonyms.

   c. Pick one of the words and write your own definition.

   d. Pick one of the words and use it in a sentence.

Odd Word Out

(Rasinski et al. 2006)

One way to make the meaning of a word clear is to compare how it is similar to or different from other words. This quick activity asks students to choose which word does not "fit" and then to explain why. It promotes classification, analysis, and creative thinking about words. Partners can work together. Their discussion of responses will be enriching. If students are all working on the same sets of words, whole-group conversation can conclude the activity.

To prepare the activity, assemble sets of four words, three of which can be grouped together for some reason, with the remaining word being the "odd word out." You may want to make activity sheets for students, such as the following:

Look at the four words. On the first line, write the one that doesn't belong. Then explain how the other words are the same.

- precook
- preheat
- premixed
- pre-test

The word that doesn't belong is _____.
The other words are similar because _____.

- prehistoric
- preshrink
- presoak
- prewash

The word that doesn't belong is _____.
The other words are similar because _____.

The groups of words you select for Odd Word Out will often have multiple answers, which will promote students' thinking about the many ways in which words can be related to one another. In the first set of words, for example, the "odd word" could be *pre-test* because the remaining words relate to cooking. Or the odd word could be *premixed* because it is the only word with an *-ed* ending. Or it could even be *preheat*, since it is the only word with a long vowel sound. It's almost better if more than one odd word can be found because it makes the activity more interesting for students.

General Procedures:

1. If the activity is new to students, you will need to introduce it. You might want to refer to *Sesame Street* and the "three of these things belong together" sketches. It may also help to show students a set of four words and then think aloud about how you might select the odd word. For example, you might put these words on the board or overhead: *cat, dog, turtle, lion*. Then you could think aloud: "The odd word could be *lion* because the other three could be pets, or because it's the only word with a long vowel sound. Or the odd word could be *turtle* because it's the only one that lives in water, or because the other three are mammals." The idea is to help students see possibilities.

2. After you have demonstrated the activity, provide another set (or two) of words and ask students to work in partners to figure out the odd word. Invite whole-group sharing. Be sure to ask students to explain their reasoning. Continue until you know that students understand the thinking process.

3. Provide students with sheets that have four to five sets of words. Each should work with a partner to figure out the odd words. Conclude with a sharing discussion, as above.

Adaptations:

1. You can differentiate instruction by providing students with different sets of words.

2. You can provide extra support for students by leading the discussion that is aimed toward finding the odd word. If you do this, be sure to encourage students' thinking rather than put ideas in their heads.

3. Students can share their words with another group without indicating their reasons for choosing the odd word. The other group tries to figure out which is the odd word.

4. If you keep words with particular roots on word walls or lists, you can invite pairs of students to examine the words to create their own sets of four words. They can explain their choices to you or, better yet, give the sets to other students to solve.

Word Theater

(Hoyt 1999)

This versatile strategy, based on the popular game of Charades, uses pantomime and oral language to make word meanings concrete. Its purpose is to help students build or reinforce conceptual knowledge by acting out the meaning of a new or familiar vocabulary word. Materials needed are a list of at least 10 words that include a root on which you wish to focus and that can be dramatized easily. Word Theater works especially well as a partner or small-group activity.

General Procedures:

1. List the words on the board or on chart paper so that everyone can see them. Tell students that they will pick one word and then work with a partner to act out its meaning without speaking.

2. Ask each student to find a partner. Each student should read the list of words to his or her partner. When both partners have read the list, they should choose a word. Tell them they have two minutes to decide how to get the word's meaning across by acting it out. Remind them that they cannot speak.

3. Now ask each team to act out its word while the other students try to guess the word they have chosen. Keep the list of words visible so that the audience can keep rereading the words as they try to figure out which one is being pantomimed. As students look for connections between the acting and the word list, they will better understand the concepts each word represents.

Adaptations:

1. Peer tutors or other more able learners, even adult volunteers, can work with young children or English language learners. In such cases, students will need more time to decide on their pantomimes. The assistant should encourage talk about the selected word as well as the actions that will become the pantomime.

2. Two sets of partners can work together if their words are related in some way. Then they can present both pantomimes together for classmates to figure out.

3. Students can make sketches instead of pantomiming.

4. Word Skits (Rasinski et al. 2006) works well with students who are both experienced in pantomiming words and comfortable working in small teams of three to four. Each team chooses one word and writes its definition on an index card. Working together, they create a skit or situation that shows the meaning of the word. The skit is performed without words. Classmates try to guess the word being shown. Once the word is correctly identified, the definition is read out loud.

Wordo

(Rasinski et al. 2006)

This vocabulary version of Bingo is a wonderful way for students to play with new words and experience the words through simultaneous use of oral and written language. Materials you will need include a list of 9 or 16 words; these may contain the same root, be related in some other way, or be randomly selected. You will also need a Wordo card for each student (a three-by-three or four-by-four square matrix; make the squares large enough for students to write in). If you would like students to use the same Wordo card several times, you will also need movable markers of some sort—dry beans, pennies, or little scraps of paper.

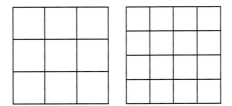

General Procedures:

1. Write the words you have chosen on the board.

2. Provide a Wordo card for each student. Ask each student to choose a free box and mark it with an X. Then have them choose words from the list on the board and write one word in each of the remaining boxes. Students choose whatever box they wish for each word.

3. Now read a clue for each word. The clue can be a definition, a synonym, an antonym, or a sentence with the target word deleted.

4. Students need to figure out the correct target word and put an X through it. (If you want to clear the sheets and play again, ask students to use movable markers.) When a

student has four Xs or markers in a row, column, diagonal, or four corners, he or she can call out, "Wordo!"

5. Check the student's words and declare that student the winner. Then have students clear their sheets and play another round. The winner of the first game can be the one to call out clues.

Adaptations:

1. For very young children or those playing for the first time, you may want to simplify the process by saying the word and then asking them to mark it.

2. A peer or volunteer can read the words aloud to beginning or struggling readers or English language learners.

3. You can play Wordo several times with the same set of words. For example, you can play a round using definitions as clues, then another round with synonyms as clues, and so forth. Afterward, you may want to engage students in discussion about which types of clues were most helpful.

4. Small groups of students can select words and develop clues. Then one group can lead Wordo for classmates.

20 Questions

The vocabulary version of this popular game uses oral language and personal connections to deepen conceptual knowledge. Students take turns asking questions that help them figure out a "mystery" word. If you want to build a little competitive spirit, you can divide the class into two teams for this activity. You will need a paper bag with at least a dozen slips of paper featuring words with a root.

General Procedures:

1. If students have never played 20 Questions, review the rules with them. Tell students that one of them will get to be "it." This student will choose a word that classmates will try to guess by asking questions. If no one can figure out the word after 20 questions have been asked, then the student who is "it" will reveal the word.

2. If someone guesses the correct word, that person becomes "it" and gets to choose the next word. Remind students that the person who is "it" can only give a yes or no answer to their questions.

3. You may want to scaffold this by taking the first turn as "it" yourself. Otherwise, invite someone to begin by selecting a word from the bag. Then let students take over and ask questions until someone has guessed the correct word.

4. Repeat the process. This game can take as much or as little time as you choose. It's good as a quick filler or Friday afternoon wind-down activity.

Adaptations:

1. You can change the number of questions that students ask. That is, you can play 15 Questions instead of 20 Questions, for example.

2. Two students can be "it" simultaneously and can confer before answering questions. This is a good adaptation for struggling readers or English language learners.

Root Word Riddles

(Rasinski et al. 2006)

This activity invites students to create and figure out riddles about words with the same root. Students guess the word by connecting clues. This works well as a partner or team activity. Required materials include chart paper, markers, and a list of at least 10 words that contain the targeted root or word part. Students will need paper and pencils.

General Procedures:

1. Begin by reviewing the meaning of the root. Read the list of words together. Ask students to explain what each word means. Make sure their explanations include the meanings of the roots.

2. If students have not created riddles before, share some riddles with them. Here are two websites with riddles to share: http://www.brownielocks.com/riddles.html or http://web.ukonline.co.uk/conker/puzzles/puzzleindex.htm

   Spend some time not only solving riddles but also talking about how riddles are constructed. Ask students what kinds of clues seem particularly helpful.

3. Now pick a word from the list and tell students you are going to create a riddle for them to figure out. Tell them you are going to give them three clues. Write out the first clue. Make sure to begin it with the words "I mean...." Then write out a second and third clue. (Example clues for the word *invisible*: I mean something you cannot see. My opposite is *visible*. I have 4 syllables. What am I?)

4. Then ask pairs of students to pick a word from the list and make their own riddle to share with the class.

5. Finally, spend some time swapping riddles. When students have written riddles about the same word, point out

the variety of clues and ways in which the word can be described.

Adaptations:

1. Students can make riddle books, perhaps by root or by word part (e.g., "Our Riddle Book of Prefixes"). These books can be added to the classroom library.

2. Volunteers or older students can partner with struggling readers or English language learners to ensure their success with the activity.

3. Students can take their riddles home for family members to solve.

4. Older students can make riddles for younger students. Riddles could be sent to students via school mail or email.

Card Games

Card games like *Memory*, or *Concentration*, *War*, and *Go Fish* are engaging independent activities. Students can play these games with decks of word cards.

General Procedures: Memory or Concentration

1. The object of this game is to find two word cards that match. To play, students will need pairs of cards with the same word, root, or word part on them. Pairs or small groups of three to four students can play this game.

2. Students should shuffle the deck of word cards and then deal them upside down. You might suggest that they make a square—four rows and four columns, for example.

3. Students take turns trying to make matches. The first student turns over two cards. If they match, the student keeps them and takes another turn. If they don't match, the student puts them back facedown, and the next student

takes a turn. The student with the most cards when all matches have been found wins the game.

Adaptations: Memory or Concentration

Students can make matches in a variety of ways:

- Prefix (or suffix) and a base word that go together to make a real word (e.g., *pre- + game = pregame* would be a match; *pre- + dog = predog* would not). You can also use words that can become compound words (e.g., *base + ball*) or that cannot become compound words (e.g., *base + lawn*).

- Words that contain the same root (e.g., *container, abstain; pre-test, preheat; look, looking*). You can challenge students by asking them to identify what the word part is or what it means.

- You can make the activity easier or more difficult by using different words and word parts.

General Procedures: Word War

1. Assemble a large deck of cards, perhaps by using brainstormed lists of words that contain certain roots (e.g., *pre-* words, *tri-* words). This game can be played with 2–4 students. You will need at least 10 word cards per student.

2. Deal the deck of word cards. (If there are leftover cards, set them aside.)

3. Each player turns a card over and says the word on it. Then all players count the letters in the word. The player with the longest word wins all the cards. Play resumes with each player turning over another card.

4. If there is a tie for longest word, those players reveal an additional card, say the word, and count the letters. These "word wars" continue until someone's word is the longest, at which point he or she takes all the cards that are turned

over. Then play resumes as in Step 3.

5. When all the cards have been turned over, the player with the most cards wins.

Adaptations: Word War

1. You can make the game easier or harder by selecting easier or more challenging words.

2. Students who need more support can play as a team: two students handling one deck of cards.

3. You can make the game more challenging by asking students to name or define word parts instead of simply saying the words on the cards that they turn over.

4. Alphabetical order rather than word length can be used to determine the first winner.

General Procedures: Go Fish

1. Assemble a deck of word cards that contains sets of four related words (e.g., *look, looks, looking, looked; return, rewind, rethink, refund; player, dancer, runner, walker*). You will need about 10 cards per player. The game can be played by 2–4 students.

2. Deal cards so that each player has seven. The remaining cards go facedown in the center of the playing area.

3. Students should sort their cards and look for related words. If dealt four related cards, these can be turned faceup on the table.

4. One student begins by asking another for a card to add to a set (e.g., "Do you have a card with the base word *look*?"). If the other student has a card that matches the criterion, he or she must give it to the student who asked.

5. The student continues asking for cards until the other student does not have one to give (i.e., does not have one that fits the criterion). At this point, the other student says, "Go fish." The first student takes a card from the center of the table. If this card allows the student to make a set of four, these go on the table and his or her turn continues. If not, this student's turn is over, and the next student takes a turn.

6. Play continues until one student has all of his or her cards in sets on the table. This student is the winner.

Adaptations: Go Fish

1. Using smaller sets of two or three cards makes the game easier.

2. Students can make their own word cards before play begins. They can begin with a list of base words.

3. Students can make matches according to prefix, suffix, or root.

Word Puzzles

Challenge students with crossword puzzles, word searches, jumbles, and word ladders. See Chapter 10 for websites that will help you make your own crossword puzzles and word searches.

Cloze

(Rasinski and Padak 2004)

This strategy is frequently used to support reading comprehension, but it is also an excellent way to model and practice using context clues to determine word meaning. Cloze activities help develop readers' understanding and use of context clues. Students predict words that have been omitted (or covered up) in a passage. To develop the activity, choose a reading selection, either fiction or nonfiction, and delete selected words.

Cloze can be done independently with activity sheets prepared in advance. It is also an excellent partner activity.

General Procedures:

1. Select a text that will challenge but not overwhelm your students. Identify several words that may easily be predicted from the semantic context of the story. Leave the first and last sentences intact so that students have a mental framework. Cover the selected words with sticky notes, or omit the words if constructing a passage for duplication. (In a pure Cloze, every fifth word is deleted, but how many and which words are omitted should depend on your judgment of text difficulty and student need, as well as the purpose of the lesson.)

2. Next, read the text to students. When you come to a covered or omitted word, finish reading the sentence before you stop. If students are reading independently, tell them to read to the end of each sentence before looking for context clues.

3. Ask students to predict the meaning of each covered or omitted word. As each word is discussed, make sure that students describe the strategies they used to figure out the correct word. This talk deepens metacognitive awareness. Point out the variety of clues that students used, as well as the importance of using prior knowledge to solve the problem.

4. After you have scaffolded Cloze several times, students will be able to complete Cloze activities independently.

Adaptations:

1. You can develop Cloze with texts that feature many examples of a particular root (e.g., many words with prefixes or a particular prefix, or with a root such as *tain*).

2. You can provide clues for deleted words (e.g., beginning sounds, base words).

3. Multiple-choice Cloze (called Maze) provides students with choices for each deletion.

4. Cloze activities can be completed on computers using cut-and-paste or click-and-drag options. This provides technology practice for students.

5. Students can develop Cloze activities for others to solve.

Scattergories

(Rasinski and Padak 2004)

This version of the popular board game is a wonderful way to use the skill of categorization to build vocabulary. The purpose of the game is to broaden students' conceptual knowledge by connecting vocabulary words to specific categories. This works especially well as a partner or team activity. To create the Scattergories matrix, put several letters along one dimension of the matrix and a list of four or five categories that can generate many words (e.g., vegetables, countries, animals). The categories can be general or developed from themes or content areas. For example:

Letters	Foods	Animals	Names
C			
F			
T			

You can also use roots. For example:

Roots	in-/im-	-ible/-able	-er/-or
port			
vis			
flam			

General Procedures:

1. Provide students with blank Scattergories matrices. Copy the matrix on the board, chart paper, or an overhead transparency. Tell students to copy one category in each box along the top. Now tell them to write the letters you have selected, putting one in each box down the side. You do the same.

2. Then tell them they have five minutes, working individually or in teams, to think of as many words as they can that begin with the given letters and fit the categories. Remind students to write all the words in one box that they think of that begin with the same letter.

3. When time is up, ask students to share their words. The player or team with the greatest number of words wins.

4. After you have scaffolded this activity several times, students will be ready to play Scattergories independently.

Adaptations:

1. Alphaboxes (Hoyt 1999) is a variation of Scattergories that can be played in teams or as a whole group. In this version, students brainstorm a word for every letter of the alphabet. The words are related to a topic or a text that has been read. (If the topic is "animals," for example, students might brainstorm *ant, bear, cat, dog, elephant,* etc.) Students can generate as many topic-related words as they can think of for each letter.

2. You can develop a Scattergories or Alphaboxes matrix for a bulletin board. Leave it up for a week and ask students to add words as they think of them.

3. Invite students to develop their own Scattergories matrices for others to solve.

Word Sorts

(Rasinski and Padak 2004)

Any activity that asks students to organize or categorize words could be called a "word sort." The purpose of any word sort activity is for students to think about different aspects of words, what the words have in common, and how they relate to a text that students have read.

General Procedures:

1. Select about 20 words for sorting. For example, you might select words that have prefixes, suffixes, or both; words that start the same but have or do not have prefixes (e.g., *preheat, press*); or words from a text that students will read. Write the words on individual cards or slips of paper. If you are introducing word sorts to students, you may also want to put the words on a blank transparency and cut them apart so that you can demonstrate the process of sorting the words.

2. Provide one set of word cards to each pair of students. Ask students to group the words. Remind them that they will be asked to explain their groupings. Some criteria for grouping include:

   - presence or absence of a prefix, base, or suffix
   - presence or absence of a particular root
   - number of syllables
   - presence or absence of a long vowel sound

   See Adaptations on the next page for additional sorting possibilities.

3. After a few minutes, invite students to discuss one of their groups, both the words contained in it and their reasons for putting these words together.

Adaptations:

1. If you are introducing word sorts, use words on bits of blank overhead to show students how to sort.

2. If time permits, ask students to sort the same set of words repeatedly (e.g., by the presence or absence of a word part, by number of syllables). Each sort provides students with another opportunity to think about both the words and their component parts.

3. If you have drawn words from a text that students will read, ask them to sort by text-related categories (e.g., characters, plot, setting). Be sure students understand that they are making good guesses, not finding the right answers, since they have not yet read the text. After reading, invite students to return to their groupings and alter them based on the text.

Summary

These activities will provide your students with interesting and engaging vocabulary practice. We recommend that you introduce one activity at a time. For English language learners and struggling students, scaffold their understanding by demonstrating the activity in a whole-group setting. Continue these demonstrations until students understand how the activity proceeds. After this, students should be able to complete the activities independently. Ask your advanced students to create new versions of these activities and to work with the rest of the class, modeling and assisting as needed.

The chart on the following page shows how adaptable these activities can be by addressing group size, whether the activities are suitable for centers (or are better for independent work), and type of words or word parts you can use.

Vocabulary Activities Chart

Activity	Group Size	Suitable for Centers	Types of Words/ Word Parts
Word Spokes	whole, small, partners	Yes	prefixes, suffixes, bases
Odd Word Out	small, partners	Yes	prefixes, suffixes, bases, general vocabulary, content-area vocabulary
Word Theater	whole	No	prefixes, suffixes, bases, general vocabulary, content-area vocabulary
Wordo	whole	No	prefixes, suffixes, bases, general vocabulary, content-area vocabulary
20 Questions	whole, small, partners	No	prefixes, suffixes, bases, general vocabulary, content-area vocabulary
Root Word Riddles	small, partners	Yes	prefixes, suffixes, bases, general vocabulary, content-area vocabulary
Card Games	small	Yes	prefixes, suffixes, bases, general vocabulary, content-area vocabulary
Word Puzzles	partners, individually	Yes	prefixes, suffixes, bases, general vocabulary, content-area vocabulary
Cloze	partners, individually	Yes	prefixes, suffixes, bases, general vocabulary, content-area vocabulary
Scattergories	small, partners	Yes	prefixes, suffixes, bases, general vocabulary, content-area vocabulary
Word Sorts	small, partners	Yes	prefixes, suffixes, bases, general vocabulary, content-area vocabulary

Chapter 6

From the Classroom: Roots in Action

In the last chapter, we shared some effective classroom-tested instructional activities that will give your students practice with roots. We noted that a good activity should provide students with practice at appropriate difficulty levels. It should provide you with ways to support students by modeling strategies, guiding assignments, leading discussions, and even participating with them in word play activities that are both fun *and* good instruction. We know that sometimes the best support comes from peers, so activities in which students can work in pairs and/or share their thoughts with others through discussion also provide excellent vocabulary practice.

As we noted, a good activity should also be "authentic," providing practice with words in many different contexts. Such practice creates an awareness of the meaning and structure of words that will fascinate students and help make them lifelong word lovers. In this chapter, we will peek in on some classroom activities where students and their teachers are learning new words—and learning about words—together!

Root of the Week

In Joanna Newton's second-grade classroom, words are everywhere. There are math and social studies word walls, as well as a student-created word wall that explores word families. One bulletin board of student writing has a bold banner that asserts, "Your Words Matter." Many of the students in Joanna's classroom have learned English as a second language. They speak a variety of first languages, including Spanish, Urdu, and Tui. She draws on their rich language backgrounds, often asking students to share words from their own countries. In fact, her students start each day with a greeting in one of the first languages of a classmate.

Joanna says her students think prefixes, bases, and suffixes are "the greatest thing on earth." She shares that one day a student joyfully observed that he loved "rocking with roots." The phrase caught on, and that is what her class now calls word study. So while some teachers may think that Latin and Greek word roots are too hard for primary-grade students, Joanna knows better.

Each Monday morning, she introduces her second graders to a new word root. After a short discussion about the root, she tapes a sheet of chart paper to a counter, writes the root at the top, and places a bowl of markers next to it. Her students spend the next few days on the lookout for words that contain the root.

They know that words from the root can appear when they read, listen, or talk to each other. They also have learned how to search for new words in dictionaries and on the Internet. Each time they discover a word that fits, Joanna's students write it on the chart paper, always initialing the entry. On Friday morning, her class assembles to review the collected words. Each student explains where he or she found the word, what it means, and how the root "gives you a clue." Classmates listen carefully to these explanations because they must decide whether the word is "real" or if they need more information to make sure.

"Root of the Week" (Newton, Padak, and Rasinski 2008) is a quick and easy way to focus attention on words that share a prefix or root word. Just post a chart with the root of the week in bold letters at the top. Number each line. Tell students that whenever they discover a word with that root, they should add it to the list. Tell them to write the word, circle the word part, and write where the word was found. At the end of the week, review the list. Students love hunting for these words, so you may find your class filling more than one sheet each week. Find a spot in the room to collect all the charts. As the weeks pass, you will have many lists of words that you can use for different purposes.

Root Word of the Day

Laura Hixenbaugh teaches fifth graders in an urban setting. For her students, vocabulary instruction has always meant memorizing spelling and definition lists, so a roots approach was unfamiliar to them. As she observes, "Students weren't *thinking* about the words and word parts. They didn't expect to be asked to think. They were used to memorizing." When she began teaching word roots, she realized that the first—and maybe most important—step in this process might be to build students' awareness of root words in their own familiar environment.

Every week, Laura and her students focus on one new root. Each day of the week, she selects a different word containing that root—one she thinks is particularly interesting or useful. This becomes the Word of the Day. Laura challenges students to use the Word of the Day as often as possible; she does this, too. Each time students hear or see the word, they raise two fingers in a V. It may look like the "V for Victory" sign, but in Laura's class, the V stands for "Vocabulary." Laura reports that the students love this activity and that it appears to have heightened their awareness of words.

There are many effective classroom approaches to Word of the Day, but we think Laura's is perfect for root study because the daily word provides an authentic semantic and linguistic context for the root. It also encourages her students to become both active listeners and articulate communicators. When they hear or use the daily word in a variety of real-life situations, students quickly come to understand that the same word can be used in many different ways. One week, for example, students are studying the root *port*, which means "to carry." On Tuesday, the daily word is *report*. One of Laura's first jobs each day is to *report* the lunch count to the office. Laura mentions that *report* cards will be coming out soon and reminds students to get their social studies *reports* in by Friday. On that day, students have heard and used *report* as a verb, an adjective, and a noun. Although in each form the word's meaning is somewhat different, they now understand that even in its many different forms, the word *report* still contains the basic meaning of "carrying" information. This is why we agree with Laura when she says the daily word helps her students "think about words and word parts."

Realia and Children's Literature

Gwen Kraeff and Sharon Milligan use primary sources, real-world artifacts (realia), and children's literature to help their students build background knowledge for a new root. Realia is often used to heighten interest, build conceptual understanding, or activate background knowledge to support students when they read a difficult text (Rasinski and Padak 2004). Here, Sharon and Gwen have used them to support students as they learn *graph/gram* ("write or draw"), an important root that appears in many abstract or conceptually difficult content-area words, including *graph, telegraph, telegram, seismograph, cardiogram, polygraph, lithograph,* and *sonogram.*

To introduce *graph/gram*, Sharon and Gwen first pass around realia of *graph/gram* words they brought in to share with their students: a *photograph* of Sharon's son; a *biography* of *Snowflake Bentley* (Martin 1998); and a *telegram, cardiogram,* and *hologram* they printed off the Internet. Sharon asks students to identify each item. As they respond, Gwen lists each word on the board. Sharon observes that this step may need scaffolding: "If they say the photograph is a 'picture,' I will help them come up with the word *photograph*." When each word is added, students are told to "discuss with their neighbor what they think the word means." When the list is finished, students are asked to figure out what all the words have in common. Students quickly notice that each word contains *graph* or *gram*, so Sharon asks them to "guess what they think *graph/gram* means."

After confirming that *graph/gram* means "write" or "draw," Sharon and Gwen tell students that *Snowflake Bentley* is a *biography* about a man who "*photographs* snowflakes." They read the fascinating tale of the "boy who loved snow" to their class, pointing out specific pages they have marked in the book that help define the word *photograph*.

This lesson gives students a chance to see concrete examples of some of the words generated by a root they are studying. We have noticed that as students become familiar with a concept, they may also bring things in to add to the teacher's realia, creating a "mini-museum for all students to see, touch, and ponder" (Rasinski and Padak 2004, 158). In following the activity with a read-aloud, Sharon and Gwen enhance their students' experience by combining word study and social studies.

Of course, no matter the topic, listening to stories is always one of the best ways to heighten interest and deepen conceptual knowledge for students of all ages. Happily, there are countless texts that can support your study of roots. Like Sharon and Gwen, you can look for texts that will scaffold conceptual knowledge about a particular root or just share lighthearted stories like *Max's Words* (Banks 2006) or *The Boy Who Loved Words* (Schotter 2006). Texts like these reveal the power of words through the adventures of young characters with whom your students will easily identify. Remember to include texts that feature word play. Even if Amelia Bedelia's word mishaps in *Amelia Bedelia's Treasury* (Parish 1995) or *Mom and Dad are Palindromes* (Shulman 2006) do not directly teach roots, they do teach students about the nature of words, an important goal of word study.

Writing an *Exciting* Story

Lara Shiplett has developed this second-grade writing activity so that her students can practice the new words they have learned with the prefix *ex-* by using them in what she calls a "creative and meaningful way." She begins by sharing an "*Exciting* Story" she has written on an overhead transparency. First she reads it to them, and then the whole class reads it together:

> With lights flashing and sirens blaring, the fire engine *exited* the firehouse quickly. The firefighters put on their fire equipment, including their breathing masks. They need to be sure to have their masks so they can inhale and *exhale* fresh air.
>
> When they got to the burning house, one of the firefighters took a tall ladder and *extended* it up the *exterior* of the home.
>
> "My dog is still in the house!" a man *exclaimed*. Hearing the man, a firefighter rushed into the burning house and found the dog. The dog was very *excited* to be returned to his owner safe and unharmed.
>
> The *excellence* of the fire department was *exhibited* when the fire was *extinguished*. The homeowner was *excited* to be safe with his dog.
>
> "Thank you, firefighters, for your *excellent* effort!" the man *exclaimed*.

As students pick out and discuss the different *ex-* words, Lara writes each one on chart paper. The class talks about her story, and she makes sure to emphasize how much she enjoyed using her imagination to come up with interesting ways to use the *ex-* words that they had learned that week. Then Lara tells them it is their turn to use their imaginations by selecting seven words from the chart and writing their own stories. She tells them that all their stories will be shared and enjoyed.

When the stories are finished, students are invited to read their selections in a "read-around." Lara reviews the rules of a read-around: whenever one person finishes, anyone can jump in and read his or her story until all the stories have been shared. She reminds her students that they cannot comment on any of the stories until all of them have been read. She also tells them to listen especially hard for the *ex-* words in order to see how many different ways the class has used them in the stories. After everyone has read, Lara makes sure that the students talk about the various stories that were created and notice "the different ways the *ex-* words were used." The students' stories are then displayed so that they can be read and enjoyed again and again.

In this activity, Lara has tailored a popular vocabulary strategy called "Story Impressions" (Blachowicz and Fisher 2006) to the study of roots. Story Impressions is a prereading strategy in which the teacher lists several key words from a story in the order in which they appear. Students are then asked to write a story using the words in that order. When the stories are finished, students read them orally. Then everyone reads the assigned text. In Lara's version, the words come from the same root, and students can use them in any order they choose.

"Authors and Illustrators" (Rasinski et al. 2006) is another variation that works well with root study. In this version, students work with a partner to write a story. Once they have finished their stories, partners trade stories with another partner team. Each team reads the new story and draws a picture to illustrate some part of it. Students then share illustrations, explaining what they drew and why they chose that part. You can tweak Authors and Illustrators for root study by inviting each team of students to brainstorm its own list of words using the root. You can also stipulate that the team draw one of the root words as part of its illustration. A discussion of their drawings is also a nice way to practice new vocabulary.

Roots Day

Rick Newton studied Latin in school, but it was "divide and conquer" word competition with homemade flash cards that truly fostered his love of English words. In "A Little Latin…and a Lot of English," (Newton and Newton 2005) Rick recalls how every week on "Roots Day," his ninth-grade Latin teacher, Miss Cassell, let her students "lay Julius Caesar aside for one hour, cast our declensions and conjugations to the wind, and just learn English vocabulary from the Latin roots":

So every Friday, "just for fun," Miss Cassell passed out 3" x 5" index cards and scissors so that we could make our own flash cards for Latin prefixes, suffixes, and bases. Wow—using scissors in Latin class—what a novelty! We were allowed to use class time to memorize our cards (what a relief—any other day of the week, this would have been a homework assignment) and then compete with one another, sometimes in teams and sometimes individually, to see who could generate the greatest number of English words from a single Latin root.

Even Miss Cassell got into the game. She created columns of words and followed each word with as many blanks as Latin roots it contained. We had to "slash" each word to identify the Latin roots and then deduce the definition. *Quadruped* had two blanks after it, so we whipped out our flash cards for *quadru* and *ped* and filled in the blanks with "four" and "foot." *Dissect* had two blanks: we filled in "cut" and "apart." *Compose* had two blanks: we filled in "put" and "together." We earned points that we could claim for extra credit toward our final grade in the course. This was serious fun!

After a month or so of these Fridays, we had an impressive stack of flash cards and some awesome vocabulary words! Just like Gus Portokalis, the father in *My Big Fat Greek Wedding*, we would go around the school and say to teachers and classmates, "Give me a word, any word, and I'll tell you it's from Latin!" Of course, we made few new friends with such sophomoric behavior (we were only freshmen!), but within our own peer group of Latin-loving nerds, we thought we had invented sliced bread.

By the end of the year, like Pavlovian dogs, we had become highly trained etymological dynamos. After all, there are only around 30 Latin prefixes. You don't even need to be a Latin student to learn them. These prefixes abound throughout our English vocabulary. For every Latin base we learned, we could generate at least 5—and often 15 or 20—English words. From *greg* (meaning "flock, herd") we formed *congregation, aggregate, gregarious, egregious, segregate,* and *desegregate*. And these were not just "dictionary words." These words appeared over and over in every course we took throughout high school and into college: words like *perturb, revoke, providential, impediment,* and *implement*. The same words showed up on the ACT and SAT. I still remember encountering *vivisect* on the SAT. I had never seen it before, but I was able to hazard an informed guess that it had something to do with "cutting" something "alive."

"Divide and conquer" was one of the slogans we learned when we read *Julius Caesar* in the ninth grade. But Miss Cassell taught us to divide and conquer vocabulary by showing us how to search for meaningful semantic units within words that may at first sight intimidate or baffle us. Indeed, some 80 percent of the words students find difficult in literature, in textbooks, and on standardized tests derive from Latin or Greek. Just having such a tool at my disposal—the habit of dividing a word into its component parts as a way of decoding its meaning—has proved to be one of the easiest and yet most powerful learning aids in my life of literacy. (If you want to read more of Rick's memoir, go to www.ohiorc.org.)

"Roots Day" is really just a variation of the popular word study activity called "Making and Writing Words" (Rasinski 2001), in which students manipulate letter cards to make new words. In this version, students are manipulating root cards to build new words.

As they flip through their flash cards to build or analyze words, roots and meanings are naturally reinforced. And because this activity can easily be done with partners or in competitive teams, students get a chance to talk about the words they are building.

Cognate Connections

In Chapter 2, we introduced the concept of cognates as an essential feature of root study: words containing the same root also have a shared meaning. We noted that cognates enable us to draw meaningful connections between certain basic words we may already know (or words that are conceptually easy) and words that are either unknown to us or more difficult to grasp. In fact, when students learn how to use cognates to figure out the meaning of new words, they have a "root awakening" that will serve them for the rest of their lives.

We began this chapter by peeking in on Joanna Newton's second-grade classroom. We end by taking a final look at a root awakening shared by two of her students, Maria and Arturo, in a guided reading group. Maria and Arturo are both English language learners. Although Maria was born in El Salvador and Arturo was born in Guatemala, they share Spanish as a first language. One morning, Joanna was preparing their group to read a nonfiction book called *The Romans,* part of the Footsteps series published by Franklin Watts, which provides an introductory tour for young readers of life in ancient Rome. Joanna asked the students to walk through the text, look at the pictures, and write three "wonder" questions they had about the ancient Romans that they thought might be answered in the book. The students then shared their wonder questions with each other.

Aqueduct was a key word in the text, and Joanna knew that aqueduct would be a new concept for her students. She also knew it was a perfect word for root study. She wrote aqueduct on the board, putting a rectangle around the root *duct*. Joanna told the group that *duct* means "to lead away." Then she asked Maria if she could use the root *duct* to predict what an aqueduct might be. Arturo immediately broke into a smile. While Maria focused intently on *duct*, he kept pointing to the first part of the word. As soon as Arturo blurted out, "agua, agua," Maria broke into a smile and said "water." Arturo explained how he knew "agua," and "aqua" must mean the same thing, because he knew many Spanish words came from Latin roots. The group then considered both roots. If *agua* and *aqua* both meant "water," and *duct* meant "lead," an *aqueduct* must be something that "leads water." They located a picture of an aqueduct in the text. Joanna told them to read the text to find out "how an aqueduct works." She also reminded them to be on the lookout for answers to their wonder questions.

We think this is a perfect example of how a roots approach empowers students. Maria and Arturo know that word parts have meaning. Moreover, they know that many word parts have come to English from other languages. Arturo also understands that you can figure out the meaning of a word by looking for cognates in all of its word parts. And because they bring the rich experience of another language to their English word study, these students have a deep linguistic background to draw upon. This "teachable moment," then, epitomizes our goal for word study: students working together as word sleuths, asking questions about meaning, and then trying to answer those questions by applying their knowledge of roots and cognates.

Summary

In the last chapter, we outlined engaging classroom-tested activities for vocabulary practice. In this chapter, we shared teacher-tested examples of vocabulary activities as they unfold in real classroom settings. Even though these vignettes highlight specific levels, all of them can be adapted to any grade level. Because they are all student centered, these activities can provide your students with practice at appropriate difficulty levels. Some of these activities build background knowledge, some scaffold difficult concepts, and some provide opportunities for students to hear, read, write, and share. All demonstrate how teachers and students can work together in ways that help students make connections between the new words they are learning and the ones they already know. In the next chapter, we will provide additional linguistic and teaching tips that may be helpful in supporting your students.

Chapter 7

Flexing with Word Parts: Some Strategies

Teachers often pose questions like these as they begin teaching vocabulary from a roots perspective:

- Once students identify the prefix and base of a word, how can we guide them into forming a definition? Sometimes students' definitions don't really make much sense because they sound so mechanical. Other times, students seem to get stuck at the prefix.

- Some roots have multiple forms. How can we help students keep them straight? For example, the base "to move" has three forms: *mov, mot,* and *mobil.* The base "to put" has the forms *pon, pos, posit,* and even *pound.*

- Some prefixes have multiple forms. How can we keep them straight? For example, the prefix "with, together" is sometimes cited in three forms: *con-, com-, col-.* How do we handle the double consonants that often appear near the beginning of a word (as in *affect, succumb, attractive,* and *collection*)? How can we guide our students to divide and conquer words like these at the right spots?

In this chapter, we provide answers to these questions and suggest some teaching strategies or routines for you to use. All of these strategies emphasize the importance of inculcating a sense of flexibility in ourselves and in our students as we approach words and their meanings—thus, the "flexing" in the title of this chapter. This sense of flexibility is important when we work with words. Although language is systematic, it is not rigid. It is a living entity produced by human beings in a variety of contexts. This is why we speak of "language arts" and not "language science."

Word Comprehension: Start with the Base, Not with the Prefix

In keeping with the phonological approach used in the primary grades, our students usually learn to pronounce a word from the front and work through it to the end. As they sound out each syllable in succession, they eventually recognize what they see and hear. This approach, though mechanical, works well when students are reading words they already know.

But the roots approach aims to expand vocabulary and introduce students to words they do not already know. For this reason, as students progress from being early decoders to being vocabulary builders, they need a new word-attack strategy to take them beyond mechanical "sounding out." We want students to come to understand that words are not just an accidental accumulation of meaningless syllabified sounds. We want them to see that word parts convey meaning. The roots approach, which is semantically based, thus calls for a realignment of the manner in which we approach word parts. As we teach students "the root of the week," we urge them to search for the *semantic unit* (not the syllabic or phonological unit) on which the word is based. Students base their understanding of the word on this base. The base unit is the core of the word, and it is not necessarily at the front of the word.

To use the roots approach to find the meaning of a word involves what we call "flexing"—loosening the way we approach the new word, if you will. We want students to become adept at flexing (and not mechanically forcing) the word parts they recognize into an understanding of the entire word.

Very often, a word's base is preceded by a prefix. This is especially so in academic vocabulary. If students try to understand a new word according to the system they learned as beginning readers—attacking it from the front and working through to the end—they will usually produce explanations that make no sense. Let's assume that the root of the week is *tract* = "pull, draw, drag" and that students are working with the word *contract*. Most students will quickly divide the word at the right spot: con/tract. Moreover, students may know that the prefix *con-* means "with, together" and the base *tract* means "pull, draw, drag." But if they combine these word parts in order of appearance, the resulting definition may come out as "with pull" or "together drag," neither of which makes sense.

You can solve this problem by asking students to "slash off" the prefix and identify the base first and then use the meaning of the base as the first word of a definition. Using *contract* as an example, students would begin with con/tract and then determine that the base is *tract*, which means "pull." Having established this core meaning, students can then add the meaning of the prefix. In other words, we want students to understand that although we read the word *contract* from left to right, we comprehend it as the base *tract*, to which the prefix *con-* has been appended. Students quickly catch on to this new skill of flexing, since their revised definition of *contract* = "pull or draw together" makes sense. When our muscles *contract*, they "draw together"; when business partners sign a *contract*, they "draw" it up "together."

You might want to use the meaning of the word *prefix* to help students understand how to apply prefixes when they are comprehending words. The Latin base *fix* means "fasten, attach." For example, business envelopes remind us to *affix* adequate postage; we are to "fasten" a stamp "to" the letter. But the letter must be there in the first place if the stamp is to be attached to it! The stamp is merely *affixed* (or attached) to something essential. Likewise, prefixes are "attachments" placed "before" the base. Prefixes exist only as attachments to the bases, and the bases provide words with their essential meanings. Like postage stamps, prefixes are not used in isolation. So it makes sense that the meaning of a word depends primarily not on its prefix but on its base. A word may often begin with a prefix, but its meaning always begins with its base.

As mentioned in Chapter 2, prefixes alter word meaning in three general ways. They may negate, specify direction, or intensify the force of the base. Most often, prefixes are directional; the prefix sends the meaning of the base in a particular direction (e.g., *under, down, with, apart, over*, etc.). Instead of asking for a formal definition, we can ask students to talk about the impact of the prefix within the context of the word's essential idea. Because Latin bases are rich in cognates, we can ask for examples of other words with the same base that carry the same core meaning. Here are some examples of "pull" words, all built on the base *tract*:

- A dentist who *extracts* a tooth "pulls" it "out." (*extract* = "pull out," not "out pull")

- Vanilla *extract* is the oily liquid "drawn out" of a vanilla bean.

- We feel "drawn to" people who are *attractive*. (*attract* = "draw to, draw toward," not "toward draw")

- When we *subtract* numbers in a column, we "draw" one number "from under" another. (*subtract* = "draw from under," not "under draw")

- A journalist *retracts* a false statement and "withdraws" it by taking or "pulling it back." (*retract* = "pull back," not "back pull")

We can also list words based on *tract* that have no prefix:

- A *tractor* is a machine that "pulls" farm equipment.

- When we *trace* a picture, we "draw" or "drag" our pencil across the paper as we follow the lines of the original picture. When we go "back" over lines we have just "drawn," we *retrace* them.

In all of these examples, we see the importance of flexibility as we use and understand the base meaning of "pull, draw, drag" in a variety of applications. A dentist literally "pulls" out a tooth by grabbing it with dental tools. In art class, we "draw" our pencil across the paper as we *trace*. When business partners "draw" up a *contract*, they are not making pictures: their "drawing" is metaphorical. When muscles *contract*, they "draw" up and tighten, just as clothes that shrink in the wash "draw" up on us when we wear them. These examples illustrate that the semantic range of a base is often quite wide and flexible, spanning literal and metaphorical realms when combined with different prefixes and used in varying contexts. Flexing word parts into meaning can be challenging, but it can also be intellectually stimulating as our students make more and more connections between words and ideas that they have never before seen as being related.

When we build vocabulary from word roots, therefore, we emphasize the base and help students see that this particular semantic unit provides a word with its core meaning. The overall teaching process involves:

- asking students to divide words into semantic parts

- helping students find bases within words and begin the definition of a word with the meaning of the base

- asking students to add the meaning of the prefix after the meaning of the base has been determined

Since each Latin base appears in many different words, all of which are cognates, you should find it easy to develop lists of words for students to examine. Begin the overall teaching process in whole-group discussions; talk students through the steps they need to take:

> "OK, now I need to find the base in this word *contract*. I see *tract*; I'll put a circle around it. I know that *tract* means 'pull or drag,' so *contract* will have something to do with pulling or dragging. *Con-*

means 'together.' Let's see—could *contract* mean 'pulling something together'? Yes, that makes sense. When people sign a *contract*, say for buying a car, they 'pull together' on the terms of the sale."

Making your thinking explicit in this manner will help students become comfortable with flexing.

After students begin to understand the thinking process that unlocks the meaning of these words, they can work together to solve a few more words. Notice that we do NOT ask students to memorize each and every derivative. Instead, the examination of multiple derivatives reinforces a conceptual understanding of a newly memorized base. Our approach does not call for memorization of vocabulary lists (since word lists are quickly forgotten). It calls for the memorization of word roots, which students "flex" into an understanding of many words, including words they may already know but may not have thought about in etymological terms. Properly taught, word roots, unlike word lists, are rarely forgotten.

Multiple Forms of Bases: Look for Core Meaning

The English language has a long and complicated history (see Chapter 9), and includes words from many different sources. The Greek and Latin languages from which we take the bulk of our academic vocabulary is highly inflected. This means that words in Latin and Greek change significantly in form as they express differences in tense (past/present/future), voice (active/passive), and part of speech (noun/adjective/verb). Although this may be challenging for students of Latin who must master the nuances of grammar, these variations pose no serious difficulty to the English vocabulary student. We simply need to hold our focus on a common core meaning of similar, but not rigidly identical, forms. Even as they vary, the different forms of Latin roots remain recognizable. Remaining flexible is key.

For example, the Latin verb (in its four principal parts) *moveo, movere, movi, motus* means "move." The participle, with its forms *motus, mota, motum*, means "having been moved." The adjective *mobilis, mobile* means "able to be moved, mobile." English has, in a sense, distilled these various forms into three core variations as it has built its own words dealing with "movement": *mov, mot, mobil*. These three forms, all sharing the foundation of *mo*, are easily recognized as being related. Such words as *movement, remove, promotion, commotion,* and *mobility* are all cognates. All students need to do is associate the concept of "movement" with all of them.

Because many Latin words have entered English through French, several bases have undergone slight spelling modifications. Such changes are often recognizable because French has a preference for vowel diphthongs (i.e., adjacent vowels produce two sounds, as in *pound*), whereas the original Latin equivalent prefers independent vowels. This is why Latin *pon, pos, posit* and the French version *pound* are cognate (observe the Latin *o* versus the French *ou*). It is beneficial for students to learn these four slightly variant forms as all dealing with the idea of "put, place": an *opponent* is someone who "puts, places" himself or herself against a challenger; we *pose* for a picture by "placing" ourselves in a flattering *position;* we produce *compounds* when we "put" two or more words "together."

The Latin bases *pung, punct,* to cite another example, mean to "pierce" and give us such words as *pungent* (smells and tastes that "pierce" our senses); *puncture* (to "pierce" a hole); *punctuation* (the periods, commas, and apostrophes that we form by "piercing" the paper with dot-like strokes); and *punctual* ("on the dot," i.e., the pierce mark). This same base has a French variant in *poign* (note the diphthong *oi*) in place of the single Latin *u*. Thus, the word *poignant* is cognate with this family: *poignant* feelings are emotionally "piercing," and we feel them keenly.

In words derived from Greek, it is common to find a connecting *o* between combined roots. This is why we find so many *o*'s in medical and technical terminology (e.g., electr-*o*-cardi-*o*-gram, pyr-*o*-phobia, dem-*o*-cracy). As we encourage our students to flex word parts, we ask them to look for *o*'s in long words (which are often Greek) and then divide and conquer the word accordingly.

Introducing this variability to students by explaining a bit of the linguistic history behind it may help them see that the forms share meaning and help them understand why this variability exists. Knowing this and being comfortable with flexible thinking can lead students to successful comprehension of bases that have multiple spellings. Helping students keep their focus on meaning is the key.

Double Consonants Within a Word: Teaching Assimilation

Some prefixes have multiple forms. For example, we find the prefix *con-* in various forms in the words *connect, combine,* and *collect*; we find variations of the prefix *ad-* in *advertise, attract, allusion,* and *affect.* Students do not need to learn each modification as a separate entity, since these slight changes follow a pattern that is recognizable and often even predictable: this is the phenomenon known as "assimilation." Assimilation simply means that some consonants change and become like ("similar to" = assimilate) the consonants that follow next within words. In this section, we will first explain what "assimilation" is and how it results in the changing or doubling of certain consonants. You may wish to read the next few paragraphs just to get the general idea. We will discuss in detail the Latin prefixes that undergo assimilation (e.g., *con-, in-, ad-, dis-, sub-, ob-*). We will then follow with a useful teaching suggestion: make it as easy as 1–2–3. The students do not need to dwell on the technical term of assimilation. By looking at sample words (which we suggest), they will get the point. If this concept is new to you as a teacher, the sample words will be likewise beneficial.

Assimilation is a common feature of many Latin prefixes. Latin prefixes, like variant forms of Latin bases, undergo spelling changes with assimilation, but the meaning does not change. These spelling changes are simply to make words easier to pronounce, which makes the language sound better. This is the principle of *euphony* (*phon* = "sound"; *eu-* = "good or well") or "sounding good." (Students do not need to dwell on this word; it suffices for them to be aware of it!) Although many consonants coexist in English words, some combinations are avoided. For example, English does not like the sound of a word like *conlect*, so it changes the *n-* of the prefix to match the first letter of the attached base. Thus, *conlect* becomes *collect*. Not only is it easier to say, but it also sounds better.

Latin prefixes that end in consonants (e.g., *con-* and *in-*) may change when they are attached to bases that begin with consonants. The final consonant of the prefix often changes into another consonant, facilitating pronunciation and enhancing euphony. In general, this change occurs only when the resulting consonant cluster would otherwise be difficult to pronounce or strike the ear as unpleasant.

When full assimilation occurs, the final *n-* of the Latin prefix often changes into the same consonant as the first letter of the base. Here are some examples:

con + lect = collect

con + motion = commotion

con + mit = commit

con + rect = correct

in + legal = illegal

in + legible = illegible

in + migrant = immigrant

When a prefix fully assimilates to match the first consonant of the base, we observe a doubling of the consonant near the beginning of the word.

Sometimes, however, the final *n-* of these prefixes fits comfortably and euphonically with the following consonant in the word, so neither spelling nor pronunciation needs to be modified. Thus, we find unaltered (or unassimilated) prefixes in such words as *concede, conference, consensus, incisive, infer,* and *ingest.*

Prefixes ending in the consonant *n-* may also assimilate the final *n-* into an *m-* if the base begins with *b* or *p.* For example:

con + bine = combine

con + pose = compose

in + bibe = imbibe

in + possible = impossible

This change is called "partial assimilation." The final *n-* of a prefix does not double into the next consonant base but only becomes an *m-* for the purposes of euphony.

Now that we have seen how assimilation occurs with prefixes ending in the consonant *n-,* let's look at the remaining few prefixes that end in other consonants. The prefix *ad-* ("to, toward, add to") has a very high degree of assimilation. Help students see that when they encounter a word beginning with *a-* followed by a double consonant, they have found an assimilated *ad-* and should look for the meaning of "to, toward, add to" in the assimilated prefix. For example:

ad + celerate = accelerate

ad + fect = affect

ad + gravate = aggravate

ad + legiance = allegiance

ad + pendix = appendix

ad + rogant = arrogant

ad + similate = assimilate

ad + tract = attract

It is important to note that the prefixes *a-*, *ab-*, and *abs-* ("away, from"), as in words like *abduct, absent, abstain,* and *abhor,* do not assimilate. Some students may confuse this prefix with its opposite, *ad-*. You may want to remind students that *ad-* always has a *d* or a double consonant, but the prefix *a-*, *ab-*, *abs-* never does.

The prefixes *dis-*, *di-* assimilate into *dif-*, but only when the base begins with *f*. Assimilated examples are *different, diffuse, diffract,* and *difficult*. Unassimilated examples of this prefix include *distribute, disqualify, disposal, divest, divulge,* and *direct*.

The Latin prefix *ob-* ("up against") also assimilates into many spellings, but fortunately, they are easily recognizable. When this prefix can be easily pronounced with the base that follows, it retains its spelling as *ob-*. Thus, we encounter such words as *obstruction* (something "built in the way" of something else), *objection* (one statement or opinion "thrown up against" another), and *obnoxious* (noticeably "harmful" or bothersome, with the sense of striking "up against" the observer).

When *ob-* assimilates, the final *b-* of the prefix consistently changes into the first consonant of the base. The result is a doubling of the consonant after the initial *o*. To divide and conquer, students simply need to divide between the doubled consonants and translate the prefix into *ob-*. With practice, students will readily recognize that most English words beginning with *opp-*, *off-*, and *occ-* contain an assimilated *ob-*. Examples:

ob + pose ("place" "up against") = oppose

ob + fer ("bring" "up against") = offer

ob + currence (a "running" "up against") = occurence

ob + press ("press" "up against" and crush) = oppress

The prefix *sub-*, like the prefix *ob-*, ends in the consonant *b*. When *sub-* assimilates, it displays the same pattern as *ob-*. English words beginning with *supp-*, *suff-*, and *succ-* contain an assimilated *sub-*. Students should look for a doubled consonant after *su-* and translate the prefix into *sub-*. Examples:

sub + fer ("bear" "up from under")	=	suffer
sub + fuse ("pour" or flush "up from under")	=	suffuse
sub + ceed ("come, move" "up from under")	=	succeed
sub + port ("carry" "up from under")	=	support
sub + press ("press" "below" and keep "under")	=	suppress

Obviously, this is much more information than your students will need in order to deal with assimilated or partially assimilated prefixes. We present it to you, though, so that you will understand the reasoning behind these spelling and pronunciation changes. Here's what we *do* want students to know:

- Although they do not need to know the rules presented in this section or all these particulars (or even the words *assimilation* or *euphony*), it will help for students to see how cumbersome it is to say words like *subport* and how easy it is to say assimilated words like *support*. We want them to understand the major reasons behind assimilation—to make words easier to say and sound better.

- Whenever a double consonant appears near the beginning of a word, students should divide the word between the doubled consonant, look for the base, and then identify the assimilated prefix.

The point is for students to be flexible when working with word parts, not define a technical term (*assimilation*) or learn a bunch of rules.

Make It as Easy as 1–2–3

You can best help students understand the concept of assimilation by using a few examples in three simple steps. In these steps, students will meet words with (1) unassimilated prefixes, followed by (2) partially assimilated prefixes, followed by

(3) fully assimilated prefixes. In just a few examples, students will readily see the progression and pick up on the pattern. In fact, assimilation is best taught by example, not explanation! Here is a suggested list of words that illustrate the three categories:

Step 1:

Using the prefixes *con-* and *in-* as examples, you might list the following:

- convention
- conference
- concur
- inaudible
- invisible
- infinite

Point out that, in these words, the final *n-* of the prefix *con-* and *in-* is easily pronounced with the next letter in the word, so no spelling change is necessary. Ask the students to say the words; they will see that all of them are easy to pronounce.

Step 2:

Using the same two prefixes, present a list of words in which the final *n-* of *in-* and *con-* turns into an *m-*. Write each word twice, first using the nonassimilated prefix and then with the partially assimilated prefix (*n-* becomes *m-*). Such words might be:

$$\begin{array}{rcl} \text{inpossible} & = & \text{impossible} \\ \text{inportant} & = & \text{important} \\ \text{conbine} & = & \text{combine} \\ \text{conplicate} & = & \text{complicate} \\ \text{conpose} & = & \text{compose} \end{array}$$

Point out that in these words, the final *n-* of the prefixes *con-* and *in-* change into an *m-* to make it easier to pronounce with the next letter. Ask the students to say each word in its nonassimilated form and then in its final form. They will readily observe and agree that in each instance, the spelling change from *n-* to *m-* makes the words sound better.

Step 3:

Now present a list of words that begin with the same prefixes (*in-*, *con-*) that demonstrate full assimilation. Write each word twice, first using the nonassimilated prefix, and then following with the fully assimilated version. In each of these examples, we will see a doubling of the first consonant:

inlegal = illegal

inresponsible = irresponsible

conloquial = colloquial

conrect = correct

As before, ask students to say each version. They will observe that the first, nonassimilated form of each word is actually quite difficult to pronounce. Then draw their attention to spelling. In every word, the final *n-* of the prefix has actually changed into the first letter of the base itself. This is why so many words in English contain a double consonant near the beginning.

After you have presented these samples to students, you might ask them to work with partners to form words by adding *con-* or *in-* to some additional bases. Students can either work with a few Latin bases they have already learned, or you can provide a few yourself. For the best results, select bases that begin with a consonant. Here are some suggestions: *tract* = "pull, draw, drag"; *pon, pos, posit, pound* = "put, place"; *mov, mot, mobil* = "move"; *grad, gress* = "step, go"; *lect* = "gather, pick"; *rect* = "straight." Students can now be asked to come up with their own words. As they produce some of the following, they should look to see if it is necessary (for ease of pronunciation) to change the spelling of the prefix:

Prefix	+	Base	=	Word
con	+	tract	=	contract (no prefix modification)
con	+	pos	=	compose (partial assimilation)
con	+	pound	=	compound (partial assimilation)
con	+	posit	=	composite (partial assimilation)
con	+	posit	=	composition (partial assimilation)
in	+	pos	=	impose (partial assimilation)
in	+	posit	=	imposition (partial assimilation)
con	+	mot	=	commotion (full assimilation)
in	+	mobil	=	immobile (full assimilation)
con	+	gress	=	congress (no prefix modification)
con	+	lect	=	collect (full assimilation)
con	+	rect	=	correct (full assimilation)
con	+	bination	=	combination (partial assimilation)
in	+	possible	=	impossible (partial assimilation)
in	+	legible	=	illegible (full assimilation)
in	+	migrant	=	immigrant (full assimilation)
in	+	finity	=	infinity (no prefix modification)

The point of this activity is to help students become comfortable with this sort of "flexing." Remember that students do not need to memorize rules or lists of assimilated words. Rather, we want them to understand that the spelling of prefixes sometimes changes to make the resulting words easier to pronounce.

How to Divide and Conquer Words with Two Prefixes

One final issue related to "flexing" has to do with words that have multiple prefixes. Here are some examples:

incorruptible   (*in-* and assimilated *con-*)

reconstruction   (*re-* and *con-*)

reproductive   (*re-* and *pro-*)

misconstrue   (*mis-* and *con-*)

The overall procedure for dividing and conquering these words is similar to the procedure for words that have single prefixes. Words with two prefixes are generally longer, of course, so it may take a bit more time for students to zero in on the base or root word. In general, we suggest the following tips:

- Advise students to identify and remove the first prefix. Using *reconstruction* as an example, students would remove the prefix *re-*.

- Ask students if the remainder of the word is recognizable. Again, with *reconstruction*, students would examine *construction* and determine that it is a recognizable word.

- Finally, students should then apply the meaning of the first prefix (i.e., the one they removed in the first step above) to the rest of the word: *re-* + construction = reconstruction: rebuilding; the process of constructing something again.

In practice, the process is not as complicated as it may first seem. For the most part, our students will be encountering "double-prefix" words that fall into two categories:

The first category includes negative forms of words they already know. These words will most frequently begin with the negative prefixes *in-*, *mis-*, or *de-*: *inadvisable, indestructible, inexplicable, irrevocable, irreversible, insubordinate; misconstrue, misinformed, misunderstand; decompose, deconstruct.*

The second category includes forms of words they already know, with the added idea of "repetition." These words will most frequently begin with the prefix *re-*: *reconstruct, reinstate, reproduce,* and *reconvene.*

Summary

We have provided information here that you need to know in order to help students with several common (but often fairly complex) problems associated with a roots approach to vocabulary learning. This technical background and terminology (e.g., partial assimilation, euphony) is important for you to be aware of, but it is not essential for our students. What do students need to know?

- Find the base. Begin defining a word by defining its base.

- Realize that some bases and some prefixes have multiple spellings.

- Be flexible!

#50472—Greek and Latin Roots   © Shell Education

Chapter 8

Digging into Dictionaries

We often hear stories about students' challenging experiences with dictionaries. Consider this scenario: a student searches in the dictionary for the meaning of the word *inequity*, only to find it defined as "lack of equity." The student still doesn't know what the word means. Now he or she has two options: look up the meaning of *equity* or read down the column until he or she finds something that makes sense. Either option can lead to even more searching, which can eventually become frustrating. This scenario may sound familiar to you—maybe you've had an experience just like this—however, this is not always the case. A dictionary can be our most trusted resource!

The truth is that most of us have probably learned very few words from the dictionary. Most often, we look up words to fulfill an immediate need, and once we locate the word and use its definition to clear up confusion, the meaning is lost. The reason for this is that it takes more than looking up a word to commit it to memory. Where the dictionary can be especially useful, then, is in exploring the rich etymologies of words—this section of the dictionary usually gets skipped over, yet it holds the greatest fascination for word lovers and is the best friend of root study.

Exploring Etymology

A quality dictionary always includes, along with the pronunciation and definition, information about the *origin*, or *etymology*, of the word. In its original Greek form, etymology means "the study of truth." When we take a moment to read the one or two lines of an entry that provide the etymology, we are led back to the root language from which the word originated.

The etymological section provides the very information that word sleuths need to divide and conquer vocabulary. It almost always identifies the prefix and base. If the dictionary editors consider it helpful, the suffix may also be identified. Each dictionary uses abbreviations that are explained on the front or back cover of the book or in an introduction at the beginning of the volume. In most dictionaries, for example, ME = Middle English, LL = Late Latin, LF = Late French, etc. By paying attention to the etymological description, we can figure out which family of cognates a word belongs to.

The etymology of words is also fascinating for our students, as they come to see that certain words are related to one another. As teachers, we want to empower students to look to the dictionary as a treasure chest of information that they can use. Our goal is to help them think about dictionaries as a way to satisfy their curiosity or confirm their hunches about words. But before they can do this, students will need to know how to explore beyond a "dictionary definition." The following are five tips to teach your students about using a dictionary for word exploration:

1. Use the dictionary to identify the roots of a word and the meaning of each part. When we introduce the Latin base *terr* ("earth"), for example, we might ask students to brainstorm words that contain this base. As they call out words, we ask them to explain what that *terr* word has to do with "earth, ground, or land." Here are some words and explanations they might come up with:

   terrarium: a container for frogs, turtles, and plants that live on the ground or on earth

   terrain: the earth we walk on; an expanse of land

   terrace: a patio that we can walk on like the ground itself

   territory: the earth that explorers investigate or that countries claim to own *extraterrestrial*: a creature from outer space, outside planet Earth (Notice how "earth" can mean ground, soil, land, and also planet Earth.)

To ensure their etymologies are correct, however, students can go to a print or electronic dictionary and look for the "word origin" section. Here's how the word *terrace* is explained in *Merriam-Webster's Online Dictionary*:

Etymology:

Middle French, platform, terrace, from Old French, from Old Occitan *terrassa*, from *terra* earth, from Latin, earth, land; akin to Latin *torrēre* to parch—more at **THIRST** Date: 1515

1 **a:** a colonnaded porch or promenade **b:** a flat roof or open platform **c:** a relatively level paved or planted area adjoining a building

According to *Merriam-Webster*, the word *terrace* comes into English from Middle French (MF), which took it from Old French (OF), which took it from Old Occitan (a French dialect), which took it from the Latin (L) word for "earth, land." (It is often the case that words from French originate in Latin. You can read more about this in the next chapter, "A Brief History of English.")

By checking the word's etymology, students can confirm that a word does indeed come from a particular root. As they associate the definition of the word with the meaning of its base, they will also come to understand that English words are not just made up of random sounds. If you have several different dictionaries in the room, you can team up the students to research the origin of words they themselves have proposed. By comparing the etymologies of their *terr* words, students quickly grasp the concept of *semantic unit* when they observe that every cognate of *terr* has an "earth, ground" meaning.

2. Use the dictionary to explore the history of a word. We first think of the dictionary as a place to go for definitions. But in addition to telling us what a word (or its roots) mean, a dictionary will also give us a short history of the word. It can answer questions about the word's origin and use over time. Because a dictionary recognizes that the meaning of a word is historically embedded, the roots approach to vocabulary engenders a new relationship between student and dictionary. Encourage your students to formulate their own questions about a word and then go to the dictionary for specific answers: "Is the word *extraterrestrial* based on the root *terr* = 'earth'?" "Where did this word come from?" "Is it an old word?"

Today there are many different kinds of dictionaries available, both print and electronic, that can provide answers to questions like these and stimulate curiosity for further word exploration. Moreover, abridged dictionaries target a range of reading or grade-level vocabulary needs. Consider having several different dictionaries (and levels) easily accessible so that students become comfortable with a variety of formats.

We believe some of the best dictionaries for students are online. These dictionaries often have appealing graphics and include easily accessible bilingual (and multilingual) forms. They may have an audio pronunciation of the word and hyperlinked text markings for immediate clarification of visual aids. Some online dictionaries focus on a particular aspect of the English language. One of our very favorites is the *Online Etymology Dictionary*, which gives a quick history of many important English words. You can add the link to your classroom computer "favorites," and students can look up the linguistic and historical roots of thousands of words. Ever wonder, for example, why the Medi*terr*anean Sea has a "land" root? A quick trip to the computer will answer your question:

Mediterranean

c.1400, from L.L. *Mediterraneum mare*
"Mediterranean Sea" (7c.), from L.
mediterraneus "midland;" original sense being
of "sea in the middle of the earth," from *medius*
"middle" + *terra* "land, earth." The O.E. name
was *Wendel-sæ*, so called for the *Vandals,* Gmc.
tribe that settled on the southwest coast of it
after the fall of Rome.

The *Mediterranean Sea*, a term of Late Latin (L.L.) origin, was so named because it was believed to be—at least in 1400—a sea that was located "in the middle (*medius*) of the earth." And here's another interesting detail: in Old English (O.E.) it had a different name, one taken from a Germanic (Gmc.) tribe that settled on its southwest coast after the fall of Rome. You need not worry if your students don't understand every word in these definitions. They will usually get the gist, and perhaps even more importantly, they will become more aware of how the meaning of a word is influenced by its usage over time.

3. Use the dictionary to reinforce "cognate connections." We call words built from the same base *cognates*, because they have been "born" (*nat*) "together" (*co-*). Cognate words enjoy an inherent and permanent relationship, one based on a shared kernel of meaning. The words *natural, nativity, native, prenatal,* and *cognate*, for example, are all in some way about "birth." When we meet a new word, we can gain a firmer grasp on it by associating it with some of its cognates. The dictionary can help us do this if we look beyond a dictionary definition.

Consider this example that introduces *varies* as a new vocabulary word: "The temperature *varies* throughout the day, warming in the morning and afternoon, and cooling at night." The linguistic context will help many students figure out that the verb *varies* must mean "change, differ." A trip to the dictionary for a definition of *varies* will confirm that meaning. But if students also ask, "What is the base of the word *varies*?" they will find that *varies* is a form of the word *vary*. They will further discover that *vary* comes from the Latin base *var*, which means "various, different." Students can now make cognate connections between the new word (*varies*) and other *var* words they may already know (e.g., *various, variant, varied, variety, variegated, variable*). Most importantly, they will see these words as semantically, not merely phonologically, related.

This "rooting" of words within their families of cognates often has a long-term payoff as well. We know that if students do not have frequent exposure to a new word, they are likely to forget it. Because the dictionary establishes each word within the context of its own family of cognates, it can support long-term language memory, even for words students only rarely encounter. Think of the *various* ways students will meet *var* words in school and beyond: In science, they may read about the *variegated* plumage of *various* birds; they will study temperature *variation* in ecology lessons; in math, they will hear about the *variables* in an equation; they may participate in a school talent show called a *variety* program; they may buy a *variety* snack pack at the grocery store. The contexts of these words will always be changing, but students' awareness of the core meaning of *var* words as "various, different" is stable and reliable. Once learned, these bases are not easily forgotten.

In Chapter 2, we observed that grasping the multiple meanings (polysemy) of a word can be confusing to students. The dictionary can also help students understand that even though the same English words can mean different things in different linguistic contexts, all of them contain a kernel of shared meaning. A *promotion* to a higher grade in school, for example, is not the same thing as a sales *promotion*. But when students ask, "What is the base of the word *promotion*?" they will discover that in each of its definitional contexts, *promotion* retains its basic meaning of "moving" (*mot*) something or someone "ahead" (*pro-*). This etymological context is more stable than the ever-shifting semantic context of words as they appear in our books.

This discussion suggests that words are in some ways like people. Throughout a single day, we find ourselves in different contexts: At home, we are parents, siblings, roommates, or neighbors; at school, we are teachers; on weekends, we may be grocery shoppers or charity volunteers. Likewise, our students are pupils in school, children and siblings at home, swimmers and dancers on the weekend, and playmates at recess. Our contexts are ever changing, but those contexts do not define us. Instead, we bring ourselves into each context as we affect others around us and as we are affected by them.

This analogy can be applied to words. We encounter words in an ever-changing range of contexts: we speak them with friends, we write them in school, we read them in novels, we sing them in songs, we study them in textbooks, and we hear them on television. But if we take a few moments when we meet a new word to trace its etymology, we can gain a firmer grasp on it by associating it with its etymological context of cognates.

4. Use the dictionary to detect "false etymology." One essential linguistic insight your students will gain is that they may sometimes make an incorrect cognate connection. Let's return to those *terr* words students were brainstorming. Here are three more they may have come up with: *terrible*, *terror*, *terrify*. While these all *look* like "earth" words, students will have difficulty explaining the notion of "land, earth" in each of these words. Now they make a trip to the dictionary with a specific question in mind: are these words associated with "earth" or not? Here is what *Merriam-Webster* tells us for *terrible*:

Main Entry: **ter·ri·ble**
Pronunciation: \ter-ə-bəl, te-rə-\
Function: *adjective*
Etymology: Middle English, from Middle French, from Latin *terribilis*, from *terrēre* to frighten—more at **TERROR**
Date: 15th century
1 **a:** exciting extreme alarm or intense fear **:** **TERRIFYING b:** formidable in nature **:** **AWESOME** <a *terrible* responsibility> **c: DIFFICULT** <in a *terrible* bind>2: **EXTREME**, **GREAT** <a *terrible* disappointment>3: extremely bad: as **a:** strongly repulsive **: OBNOXIOUS** <a *terrible* smell> **b:** notably unattractive or objectionable <*terrible* behavior> **c:** of very poor quality <a *terrible* movie

In fact, these are not "earth" words at all. There is another family of words based on the root *terr* that deal with fear. The dictionary definition of *terrible* suggests that we also look up the word *terror*. If we do, we will find even more cognates from this base.

False etymologies teach us that language is complex. If we can help students feel comfortable with this complexity, they will approach learning new words as a strategic process. Too often, particularly in school, students view learning as a pursuit of the single right answer. While root study is also about the pursuit of a right answer, the process of exploring how language works helps students become agile wordsmiths. It is also this complexity that makes language so interesting—and the dictionary so helpful.

5. Use the dictionary to nurture word curiosity. Finally, we urge you to build the dictionary habit in your students through word exploration activities. Here's a final *terr* word, *terrier*, that you might use in a word research game. Most of your students will know that a terrier is a breed of dog.

But if you ask them whether the meaning of *terrier* comes from the "earth" or "fear" form of *terr*, they may be puzzled. The etymology is not obvious. Some students may think "fear" because terriers try to scare us with their barking and snarling. This seems to make sense, but is it right? Is this a correct etymology or is it a false etymology? Even we teachers may not know for sure. So we go to the dictionary to find out. Is *terrier* an "earth" word or a "fear" word? The *Online Etymology Dictionary* tells us:

> **terrier**
> c.1440, from O.Fr. *chien terrier* "terrier dog,"
> lit. "earth dog," from M.L. *terrarius* "of earth,"
> from L. *terra* "earth" (see *terrain*). So called
> because the dogs pursue their quarry (foxes,
> badgers, etc.) into their burrows.

Those little dogs are not "terrifying," at least not to us humans, but they do burrow into the earth as they pursue other animals. By presenting vocabulary in this way and by looking to the dictionary to figure out a word's origin, we pique our students' curiosity. We also acquire the confidence we, as teachers, need when we explain word meanings to the class: sometimes, etymologies can be tricky, but the dictionary assures us that we understand the word correctly. As students take the time to focus on what a word means, they make logical connections between members of related root families: the word *terrier*, they learn, is cognate with *terrarium*! Students also learn that each word has its own history and background. Although dictionaries may not appear fascinating, they contain a lot of information that is!

Choosing and Using Dictionaries

Because the English language is perpetually evolving (language is really a living entity), new words emerge on a daily basis. As a result, no dictionary claims to be complete or even infallible. Some dictionaries opt to omit certain words that editors, for whatever reasons, deem inappropriate. Years ago, the contraction "ain't" was omitted by language purists (called "prescriptivists") who believe that dictionaries should include only "legitimate" words. Other editors, however, maintain that dictionaries should describe language as it is used and include slang or nonstandard items: such editors advocate a "descriptivist" approach.

In addition, many words change in meaning over time. A dictionary published before 1990, for example, may define the word *postal* as "of or pertaining to the post office or mail service." A more recent (and descriptivist) one might include the phrase *go postal* as colloquial or slang for "go violently berserk." This is one of the reasons why having a variety of dictionaries in a classroom can be helpful: they can stimulate discussion about words and raise questions about when it is appropriate to use or avoid certain terms and phrases. This is also why online versions provide added interest and value: they can update word lists and definitions much more quickly than hard copies.

How, then, do you choose the right dictionaries for your classroom? When considering a particular dictionary, it is a good idea to check for comprehensibility and clarity: Are the definitions and explanations easily understandable? Can your students understand them? Some dictionaries may be targeted to young readers and be particularly age appropriate for your students. Consider looking up the same word in a variety of dictionaries to see which is the most clear. Imagine your students looking up the same words. Would they understand the definitions? The following are a few extra tips to keep in mind when choosing and using dictionaries.

1. Usage Notes. Most dictionaries qualify particular words and definitions with usage notes that describe some unique way in which a word is used. Some usage notes, for example, may differentiate definitions as uniquely American or uniquely British: *corn* in British usage means what Americans understand as *wheat; biscuit* means *cookie* in British usage, which is different from the American usage of the word.

Alternate spellings may be provided (*adviser* vs. *advisor*), with some spellings marked as distinctly British or American.

Usage notes may also indicate if a particular word or meaning is *colloquial:* this means that the word is proper and acceptable in spoken English (or in direct dialogue in written texts) but should not be used in formal writing. A word or definition marked as *informal* is appropriate in casual speech, creative writing, letters, and other familiar settings, but should be avoided in formal speaking or writing. If a word is marked as *slang, nonstandard,* or *substandard*, it is to be avoided in circles that demand proper speech. (Such recommendations of usage are often, of course, a matter of opinion. Dictionary editors consult closely with teachers and other word experts in formulating these opinions.)

Words and definitions identified as *archaic* are used only rarely and invoke an older period. Such words as *thee, thou, thine, hath,* and *ye* may be termed "archaisms" in some dictionaries. These words may be encountered in church rituals or traditional hymns but would sound out of place anywhere else. Sometimes a word has an archaic meaning that is strikingly different from its current meaning. While the word *egregious* means "flagrant, notorious, outstandingly noticeable in a negative sense" in current English, it has an *archaic* definition of "distinguished and eminent." Words marked as *obsolete* have fallen into total disuse and are likely to be encountered only in extremely old sources.

2. Run-on Entries: To save space, many dictionaries include "run-on entries" or additional forms of a word. They are often listed in bold print and appear at the end of the definition of a closely related word. For example, the adjective *bearable* has its own entry in most dictionaries. At the end of the definition, however, the noun form *bearableness* and the adverbial form *bearably* are added as run-ons because these forms are not listed or defined independently. Similarly,

the noun *impoverishment* may not be found as its own entry but as a run-on placed at the end of the entry for the verb *impoverish.*

3. Etymological information may not be given for every word in order to save more space. The *Random House Webster's College Dictionary*, for example, etymologizes the verb *educate* as deriving from Latin *educatus, -ate*, which means "brought up, taught." (This is the verb the Romans used to describe the raising of children who were "led out" of childhood as they were taught by their tutors.) This information is not repeated for the closely associated words that appear on the same page: *educable, educated, education, educational, educationist, educative, educator, educatory.* Editors assume that readers will know to look for the main word with which other forms are closely associated. They assume, it seems, that readers will be word sleuths! Since the prefix and base of these words are the same, their etymologies remain unaltered.

4. Many dictionaries also omit etymologies for the negative form of words that have a positive counterpart. In the beginning of this chapter, we cited the word *inequity* and its definition in one dictionary, "lack of equity." This particular dictionary hereby instructs the reader to look up *equity*, which *does* include the etymology from Latin *(a)equitas* = "equality, fairness." It is important to raise our students' awareness of these features so that we can get the most out of the dictionaries we use.

Summary

What *are* dictionaries good for? We hope we have convinced you that they are good for just about anything and everything we want or need to know about words. We simply must know what questions to ask of them and where to find our answers. We should not rely on them only in moments of despair (although they are good for that, too!). Instead, we should turn to them as we cultivate an interest in words for words' sake, looking to see the connections between the many words we already know and the many more we will always be learning.

Those connections are often so evident (e.g., *terrarium* and *terrace)* that we do not think of them unless we take a moment to go sleuthing. Once we start thinking in terms of word origin, we start asking new questions (e.g., Is a *terrier* an earth dog or a frightening dog?). These questions now become fascinating to us rather than tedious. The dictionary answers all of our questions and builds our confidence as we continue to think actively about vocabulary.

Furthermore, since none of us knows the roots and etymologies of all the words we use and teach, dictionaries can help us become confident teachers of English vocabulary. More importantly, they can build confidence in our students. Whenever we meet a new word or our students suggest a cognate we are unsure of, we can say, "Let's look it up in the dictionary." The paradigm has shifted. The old imperative we used to dread, "Look it up!" has now become an invitation to explore the interesting histories of the words in our language.

#50472—Greek and Latin Roots © Shell Education

Chapter 9

A Brief History of English

Knowing one's history is important, whether it is personal, family, community, or cultural history. Knowledge of where we have been can help us better understand who and where we are today and perhaps provide insights into what the future may hold. Languages have interesting histories as well. English, in particular, has a fascinating history. In fact, it has multiple histories because it has multiple sources. These various sources have informed and profoundly influenced the English we speak, read, and write today.

Before we set out on our brief tour of English, here are some interesting facts about the language. Of the thousands of languages spoken around the world, English is arguably the most pervasive. It is the international language of business, government, technology, science, and the arts. It is spoken and read on six continents and is an important language in well over 80 countries (Brook 1998). It is spoken by more than a billion people. Even in countries with no significant historical ties to England or the United States, the study of English is often a requirement for high-school graduation. Many universities throughout the world insist on a perfunctory knowledge of English for admission into undergraduate and graduate programs. They also require advanced study of English at the college level, since it is assumed that educated professionals will be coming into contact with written and spoken English throughout their careers. On an international level, business and diplomatic transactions between people of different countries are often conducted in English as the "lingua franca," or common language. Worldwide, the English language is associated with education, progress, commerce, diplomacy, and advancement on many levels.

Not only is English a widely used language around the globe, it is also a deep language. By deep, we mean that it has more words than any other modern language (Brook 1998). English has more than a billion words, although only about a fifth of them are used regularly. Still, that is more than double the number of words used on a regular basis in many of the Romance languages, to cite just one linguistic family. The rich depth of the English vocabulary is directly attributable to its breadth: English speakers who have come into contact with other cultures throughout modern history (through travel, trade, cultural exchanges, and military conquests) have absorbed artifacts, products, concepts, and modes of expression into their own language. It would be fair to suggest that the English vocabulary is a melting pot of words from around the world. Did you know, for example, that we took the word *ketchup* from the Chinese, the word *chocolate* from Native Americans, the word *algebra* from Arabic, and the word *khaki* from the Persians (inhabitants of modern-day Iran)? Speakers of English have proven to be excellent listeners and adaptors, freely taking new words into this ever-growing language family. But the most significant contributors to the English vocabulary have been the ancient Greeks and Romans. In this chapter, we explain how two erroneously named "dead languages" came to provide more than 70 percent of the words in an English dictionary and more than 90 percent of English words of two or more syllables!

These few facts provide those of us who teach English with some important insights. First, we see that a solid grounding in English, in its spoken and written forms, is important both for our students and for us who, as teachers, aim to model lifelong learning for our students. For students to be successful in school and in their adult life beyond the years of their formal education, they must learn English—and they must learn it well. Second, the broad scope and deep history of the English vocabulary mean that an English-speaking student has a daunting number of words to master. Teachers are charged with the instruction of literally thousands of words that are essential to an understanding of all the content areas in a curriculum: history, politics, government, the natural sciences, mathematics, literature, the humanities, technology, the fine arts, and even the vocational arts. Without the words, students cannot learn the material. The very richness of English thus poses special challenges for students and teachers alike. Students in foreign countries may be able to function with a few words and phrases from a single discipline. But our students must master the entire word system. Herein lies our challenge, but herein also lies the attraction—for words are not only important, they are also intrinsically interesting. As we broaden and deepen our own and our students' vocabularies, we become increasingly "word conscious," or interested in vocabulary for vocabulary's sake. The ancient Greek statesman and philosopher Solon of Athens (594 B.C.) wrote, "I grow old ever learning." This adage applies to everyone, but most of all to teachers themselves. Our language is ever evolving, adding new words every day. We, too, are perpetually learning. But how did our language come about?

The Romano-Celtic Period: 55 B.C.–A.D. 410

Despite its current importance, English comes from humble origins. The history of English is largely a history of England itself and the peoples who came to that island from the western coast of Europe (McCrum, Cran, and MacNeil 1987). The original settlers of England were the Celts, descendants of people who now live in Scotland, Ireland, Wales, and Brittany in France. The Celts, who spoke a language known as Gaelic, had been living in England for several hundred years when Julius Caesar and his Roman legions invaded Gaul (modern-day Switzerland and France) in 55 B.C. By the first century A.D., the Romans had crossed the British Channel and occupied Britain as well. Unable to conquer the entire British Isle and attempting to fend off the hostile Celts to the north, the emperor Hadrian erected Hadrian's Wall in A.D. 125, thereby putting an end to Rome's northward territorial expansion. The Romans remained in England until 410, when they withdrew their last appointed governing official.

This 400-year period was crucial to the linguistic development of the people whose descendants would eventually become speakers of modern English. When the Romans occupied Gaul and Britain, they brought with them their own language, Latin. Especially in cities and towns, Latin was imposed as the language of public administration and also became the language of everyday communication. As the Roman soldiers commingled with the indigenous populations, the so-called "Romance languages" (i.e., Roman based) were born: French, Italian, Portuguese, Romanian, and Spanish. The military nature of this commingling is still evident in such place names as Greenwich ("Green Village": the suffix -*wich* is from Latin *vicus*, meaning "village" [think of the word *vicar*]) and Winchester ("Win Camp": the suffix -*chester* is from Latin *castra*, meaning "camp"). In outlying areas and in the countryside, by contrast, the native people spoke their own various Celtic dialects, resulting in a peaceful coexistence of two language groups. The very name of London (ancient Lugdunum) is derived from the Celtic word *dunum*, meaning "hill fortress" (think of high sand *dunes*).

During this bilingual Romano-Celtic period, a pattern emerged: the Celtic dialects provided the names of common and familiar everyday objects and places, while Latin provided the names for the many inventions and technological advancements that the Romans brought with them. For the most part, the Celtic words were monosyllabic, while Latin—a highly inflected language—provided the longer words. Outstanding engineers, the Romans built paved roads wherever they went (which is why we say "all roads lead to Rome"). They constructed elaborate aqueducts to bring potable water from the mountains into public living areas. As they expanded the economy, they built large villas (a Latin word) to oversee the farmers who worked the estates. The crops they produced would be consumed not only by the locals, but also exported to other parts of the empire. All these new things introduced by the Romans also brought in new words. Thus, along with the Roman roads themselves, the Latin word for paved street, *via strata*, came into the Romance languages (e.g., Italian *strada*) and also into English (*street*). The indigenous populations had never seen aqueducts or villas before. Their vocabularies expanded as the Romans modernized their lives.

But the Romans brought more than roads, aqueducts, villas, and armies into Britain. They also brought the cultural inheritance of the Greeks. When Rome defeated ancient Greece and reduced it to the status of a province in 144 B.C., the victor confessed, "We have conquered Greece, but Greece has imposed her arts on rustic Latium." The earliest example of Roman literature (273 B.C.) was a Latin translation of Homer's *Odyssey*, intended for use as a text for Roman schoolchildren. The same translator, a slave named Livius Andronicus, also translated Greek plays into Latin so that the Romans could enjoy them. In the visual arts, Roman sculptors learned their skills by making copies of Greek statues. The study of ancient Roman culture is, in many ways, the study of the translation of Greek culture into Latin. Nearly all of the various disciplines that lie at the core of any educational system today can be traced back to Greece: the words *school, poetry, drama, tragedy, comedy, theater, philosophy, theology, history, technology, biology, chemistry, physics, geometry, anatomy, astronomy, mathematics, biography, politics,* and *democracy* are all derived from Greek. Thus, when the Romans occupied the Western world, they brought in a Greco-Roman culture that had words for things that the indigenous populations had never even imagined. This is why the so-called "higher pursuits" of education are directly connected to an understanding of the Greek and Latin foundation of English vocabulary. The word *translate* is from Latin, meaning "to carry across." The Romans were *translators* in every sense of the word. They carried Greek culture into Latin, and they carried this culture into Europe and England. This is why more than 70 percent of the words in an English dictionary are from Greek and Latin bases, and why more than 90 percent of all English words of two or more syllables are of the same classical origins.

Old English: 450–1066

In the middle of the fourth century A.D., West Germanic tribes who spoke a Low German dialect akin to modern Saxon moved into the areas occupied by the Romans and the Celts. In 450, after a series of pirate raids along the British coast, these tribes of Angles (who eventually gave their name to England), Saxons (hence the term *Anglo-Saxon*), and Jutes occupied Britain and established the first Germanic settlement there. They called this area the Kingdom of Kent. The original Celts were driven to the fringes of Scotland and Wales, to nearby Ireland, and to Brittany on continental Europe. It is in the commingling of the Anglo-Saxon invaders of Britain with the now-Romanized culture they found there (with its Greek- and Latin-based vocabulary) that the English language was born. We call this initial stage Old English. It may interest you to know that in many American universities during the first half of the twentieth century, students who aspired to become English teachers were required to take courses in German and Latin; the structure of English (its syntax, grammar, and pronunciation) is Germanic, but its vocabulary is Greco-Roman.

As we observed in our discussion of the Romano-Celtic period, a pattern similarly evolved during the Old English period. Most of the common words used in the daily lives of the Angles, Saxons, and Jutes come from the Germanic roots of English. Words—again, primarily monosyllabic—such as *fire, fight, high, knob, foot, knuckle, knee, wrist, hate, wrong, help, love, meat, we, wife, sheep, ox, earth, hill, land, dog, wood, field, work, sun, moon, here,* and *there* come from the original Anglo-Saxon-Jute invasion of England. Latinate vocabulary, by contrast, was used for words of higher concern. Saint Augustine brought Christianity to the island in 597. As with the original Romans under Julius Caesar, a building program ensued. Churches and monasteries were erected, and clergy were imported. Besides serving as places of worship, these buildings also housed students and educators. The first classical curricula were established in such disciplines as poetry, grammar, astronomy, mathematics, and rhetoric. (This is why many college and university campuses resemble cloistered monasteries and the academic regalia of caps and gowns recall early Christian monks.) Much of this instruction was conducted in Latin and, to a lesser extent, in Greek and Hebrew. In the late fourth century, St. Jerome translated the original Greek and Hebrew Bible into Latin: this is known as the Vulgate Bible, meaning "the Bible for the masses," and it was used as a language textbook by educators as well as a source of religious instruction. Such church-related words as *altar, ark, candle, cross, crucify, inundation* (from Noah and the flood), *congregation, mass, minister, disciple, redemption, sacrifice, shrine, silk, priest, bishop, vestments, temple,* and *beatitude* come from the Latin Vulgate. Also included in this list are many Greek-based words that were translated into Latin: words like *angel, apostle, epistle, psalter,* and *psalms.* Hebrew words such as *Sabbath* and words of Middle Eastern origin such as *camel, cedar,* and *myrrh* were also integrated into English. Once again, we observe the profound effect of linguistic and cultural translation on the creation and growth of the English language. The advent of Christianity in England had an impact even on some of the original Germanic words brought by the Angles, Saxons, and Jutes. The words *God, heaven,* and *hell* are Germanic words that took on deeper meaning with Christianity. The Greek word *evangelium,* which means "good news," was transformed into the Germanic *god-spell,* from which our word *gospel* comes. Similarly, the Latin *Spiritus Sanctus,* which means Holy Spirit, became the Germanic *Halig Gast,* which eventually evolved into *Holy Ghost.*

Although the invasion of the British Isles by the Angles, Saxons, and Jutes led to the birth of English, the English that evolved would be scarcely recognizable to English speakers of today. One of the greatest impetuses to the evolution of English came from the other peoples and their languages that touched English. When other people invaded England, they brought their own languages that melded with the English that was spoken at the time to make a new form of English.

The Angles, Saxons, and Jutes were not the last to conquer and settle in England. More invasions were to follow. Next were the Scandinavians, also known as Vikings, Norsemen, or Danes, who began to arrive in 787. The Danes occupied the northern part of England, leaving the southern part to remain predominantly Germanic or Anglo-Saxon. Until 1050, the Danes intermarried and mixed with the Anglo-Saxons, leading to a mixing of the two languages. Unlike the Celts, who were vanquished and whose language had little impact on the language brought over by the Anglo-Saxons, the Anglo-Saxons created a form of English that did not disappear. This version of English was greatly influenced by the Scandinavian language of the Danes. English words such as *hit, leg, low, root, scalp, scatter, scare, scold, scrape, skin, skirt, skit, sky, same, want,* and *wrong* are all of Scandinavian descent. Again we observe that these words are largely monosyllabic and refer to daily things and events.

The most important text in Old English is the epic tale of *Beowolf.* Here are its first three lines. Can you read them?

> HWÆT, WE GAR-DEna in geardagum,
> þeodcyninga þrym gefrunon,
> hu ða æþelingas ellen fremedon!

(http://www.fordham.edu/halsall/basis/beowulf-oe.html)

Neither can we, but here is a translation by Francis Gummere:

> LO, praise of the prowess of people-kings
> of spear-armed Danes, in days long sped,
> we have heard, and what honor the athelings won!

(http://www.fordham.edu/halsall/basis/beowulf.html)

The marriage and evolution of the Germanic and the Scandinavian languages in England, from approximately 500 to 1200, gave rise to Old English. However, a new conquest of England was about to occur that would change the language once again. This one did not come from the north, but from the south.

Middle English: 1066–1500

In 1066, the Normans from France defeated King Harold and the Anglo-Saxon English at the Battle of Hastings, initiating a new phase in the development of English. King Harold was the last English-speaking ruler of England for nearly 300 years. The Norman French, led by King William, took complete control of the English government. For the next several generations, official activities were conducted in French. But let us recall that French itself is a Romance language, the product of Julius Caesar's original conquest of Gaul and the subsequent commingling of Roman soldiers with the local inhabitants. Many English words that refer to the government and the law are of French origin, and they entered the English language during the Norman conquest of England. Words such as *authority, attorney, council, empire, felony, judge, jury, liberty, mayor, nobility, parliament, prince, treaty,* and *treasurer* are derived from French words that themselves are of Latin origin. Thus, during the period in which Middle English evolved, we see a doubling of the impact of Latin: the Latin of Julius Caesar's troops, followed by the latinized French of the Norman invaders and law givers.

By this time, the Latin language had been well established as the principal language in which the affairs of religion and the Christian church were conducted. Since most formal education was conducted through the church, Latin remained the language of education and academia. The enrichment of the English vocabulary by Greco-Latin words was continuing, and the role of Greco-Latin vocabulary as the language of education was here to stay. The common people of England, the original Anglo-Saxons, continued to speak in their original language while learning, unavoidably, some French. The French rulers relied on their native language, while learning only enough English to give orders to their English subjects. The English speakers, by contrast, were absorbing all these words, which were, for the most part, of Latin origin. Imagine how rich the linguistic environment of England was during this period!

Three languages were in use at one time, spoken and written for three distinct purposes—French for government, Latin (and translated Greek) for religion and education, and indigenous English for everyday conversation.

As for English itself, its structure and syntax remained largely unchanged as an Anglo-Saxon tongue. But with its longstanding tradition of openness to other cultures, its vocabulary grew exponentially as it absorbed the cultural influences of the Latin-speaking church and the French overlords. This is one of the most remarkable features of our language. We have different words from different sources to express a wide range of concepts on various "levels of discourse." Although this intermingling of languages has resulted in a complicated language in terms of pronunciation and spelling (for example, the silent *k* in the words *knight* and *knee* and the British spelling of *colour*), it has also resulted in an English that is rich in its ability to communicate shades of meaning. One concept can often be expressed in different ways in English, each reflecting a different language source. For example, the Anglo-Saxon *fear* can be expressed as *terror* in French (originally Latin), and *trepidation* in Latin. In many cases, these semantically related words carry a difference in sense. For example, the monosyllabic *win* in Anglo-Saxon is an all-purpose word (e.g., we can *win* the lottery, *win* a race, or cultivate charming and *winning* ways). The French-based equivalent, *succeed,* means literally "to come up from under" (e.g., one king *succeeds* another; an American *success* story about a poor boy or girl who makes a fortune). The Latin *triumph* carries a connotation of swaggering after a major victory, or overcoming an extremely formidable foe. Anglo-Saxon *kingly* can also be communicated as *royal* and *sovereign* in French and as *regal* in Latin. We thus have the option of any number of expressions: we can speak of a *kingly* demeanor, a *royal* feast fit for a king, a *sovereign* ruler, and the *regal* furnishings of a palace or someone's sumptuous living room. Clearly, although French and Latin have made the original Anglo-Saxon English much more complex, the ability to communicate with deeper and more subtle nuances has been enhanced through the adoption of these culturally rich vocabularies.

Although the French Normans ruled lands in France and England after the Battle of Hastings, by the early thirteenth century landholders in both countries were forced to declare their allegiance to either France or England. In 1244, the King of France pronounced that "as it is impossible that any man living in my kingdom, and having possessions in England, can competently serve two masters, he must either inseparably attach himself to me or to the King of England." This separation meant that although French-speaking men of French origin may still rule England, their ultimate allegiance must now be to England, not France. Thus, the French language, although well established in England, did not supplant the Anglo-Saxon English spoken by the everyday people.

The sense of nationalism that arose as the nobility in England declared themselves Englishmen or Frenchmen, combined with the Hundred Years War (1337–1454), allowed Anglo-Saxon English to remain the dominant language of the island. But the English that evolved during this period—now called Middle English—incorporated the rich French and Latin vocabulary of the occupier. In 1356, when the mayor of London declared that all court proceedings were to be held in English instead of French, the English language itself was replete with borrowed words that dealt with law, government, and other official dealings. Furthermore, in 1362, the transactions of the British Parliament were conducted in English, not French. During the rise of Middle English, therefore, Latin vocabulary embedded itself even more deeply.

Geoffrey Chaucer (1343–1400), who wrote *The Canterbury Tales*, lived during this time. Here are the first several lines from "The Knight's Tale." As you will see, they're written in Middle English. See if you can figure them out. (The translation is provided at the end of the chapter.)

Whilom, as olde stories tellen us,
Ther was a duc that highte Theseus;
Of Atthenes he was lord and governour,
And in his tyme swich a conquerour
That gretter was ther noon under the sonne.

(http://www.courses.fas.harvard.edu/~chaucer/teachslf/kt-par1.htm)

How did you do? Was this easier to read than the Old English excerpt from *Beowulf*? What do you notice about Middle English word order? Do you see what might be a French influence on spelling?

The stage was now set for the Renaissance.

Modern English: 1550–present

The beginning of modern English can be traced to the Renaissance. The term *Renaissance*—a French word of Latin origin—means "rebirth" and refers to the rediscovery of the ancient western civilizations of Greece and Rome. Beginning in Italy, the reawakening of intellectual interest in the cultural achievements of the classical Greeks in particular quickly spread throughout Europe and into England. The Renaissance was an exciting period of science, invention, discovery, literature, and exploration for the entire Western world. The Renaissance reintroduced Europe to the scientific knowledge and writings of the Greeks and Romans. Thus, English was given a third exposure to Latin. This time, however, the European scholars were not content to rely on Latin translations of the works they were studying. They insisted on returning to the Greek language itself. This is how so many Greek-based words of science and technology were introduced into English. Students of medicine and anatomy returned to the original writings of the ancient Greek Hippocrates, the father of medicine. Students of geometry began reading Euclid in the original Greek. Philosophers and theologians turned to Plato and Aristotle, while poets and dramatists read Homer, Sophocles, and Euripides in ancient Greek. Such academic, scientific, technical, and medical words as *atmosphere, atom, catalyst, analysis, trigonometry, trapezoid, capsule, catastrophe, lexicon, pneumonia, skeleton,* and *thermometer* come directly from Greek. By the eighteenth century, European and British scholars were so taken with the study of Greece that a new intellectual movement began, Philhellenism, which means "the love of things Greek." British poet Percy Bysshe Shelley (1792–1822) wrote in his *Preface to Hellas,* "We are all Greeks. Our laws, our literature, our religion, our arts have their roots in Greece." This is an amazing statement by an Englishman who found his intellectual identity in the study of Greece. The English people and the English language have an age-old tradition of respecting, adopting, and transmitting the legacies of Greece and Rome.

Words from other lands and languages that were immersed in the Renaissance also influenced English. From French came more words such as *bigot* and *detail,* from Italian came *portico* and *stucco,* from Spanish words such as *desperado* and *embargo,* and from the Low Countries came *smuggle* and *reef.* The Renaissance was indeed a time of new words for English. During this period, between 10,000 and 12,000 words were added to the language.

In 1476, the printing press was introduced into England by William Caxton. Books became less expensive and more abundant. Between 1500 and 1640, 20,000 books, pamphlets, and broadsheets were published, a 50 percent increase over what had been published in all of Europe before 1500. Thus, an ever-increasing number of English people were learning to read and write. English was spreading, not only in terms of number of words, but also as a written and oral language that was used by a growing number of people. In 1604, King James commissioned a new translation of the Bible into English. The English vocabulary that appears in this text owes its very existence to the Vulgate Latin Bible that St. Jerome had produced some 1200 years earlier. By now, the effect of Greek and Latin vocabulary had made an indelible impression on the English language. From the King

James Bible come several expressions that are current even today: *the apple of his eye, salt of the earth, fruit of the womb, out of the mouths of babes,* and *baptism by fire.* This level of English was not restricted to those who could read and write. The sacred texts were read aloud during church services, and the English speaking public absorbed all this rich vocabulary simply by listening.

Besides the King James version (*version* means "translation") of the Bible, another cultural marvel appeared as Modern English was being born: William Shakespeare (1564–1616). With his tragedies, comedies, poems, and sonnets, Shakespeare entertained both the nobility and the masses with his enormous talent for "neologizing." He actually created new words in English. He used nearly 18,000 different words in his entire body of work, a remarkable range of vocabulary for his time. Of these words, close to 10 percent were of his own invention. Shakespeare's education included training in the classics and rhetoric, both of which are rooted in the Latin and Greek languages. In particular, he was fascinated with classical myths as recorded in the Roman poet Ovid's long poem, *Metamorphoses,* to which he turned for inspiration for many of his plots. Shakespeare was also an avid reader of Latin poetry. Thus, we find yet another instance of the impact of Latin on English. When Shakespeare coined new words, he combined the already-existing Latin and Greek roots that he knew by heart. Words such as *baseless, dishearten, dislocate, impartial, indistinguishable, invulnerable, lonely, metamorphosis, monumental, premeditated, reliance, sanctimonious,* and *submerge* are examples of the many words Shakespeare created to express meaning and engage his language-sensitive listeners.

Following are the first few lines of Hamlet's famous soliloquy, "To be or not to be" from Shakespeare's *Hamlet.* Although you have probably seen and studied these lines many times in the past, this time we ask you to look at the language. We guess that this will be much easier for you to read than *The Canterbury Tales.* Why? How do words and word order compare to Middle English? What evidence do you find of figurative language?

To be or not to be, that is the question;
Whether 'tis nobler in the mind to suffer
The slings and arrows of outrageous fortune,
Or to take arms against a sea of troubles,
And by opposing, end them.

(*Hamlet*, *Shakespeare*, Act III, scene ii)

The New World: English on the Move

The history of English is not only the story of the various people who invaded England and brought their languages with them. It also the story of English-speaking people traveling and emigrating abroad and acquiring words from the speakers of the lands they visited. The Renaissance was not only a time of rebirth of the ancient Greek and Roman classics; it was also the time period during which England emerged as a world-class maritime power, surpassing the Spanish. The English people and their language began moving out and making their way into other lands around the globe.

A large part of this cultural, political, and commercial expansion focused on the original American colonies of the New World, beginning with the settlement of Jamestown, Virginia, by the London Company in 1607. In 1620, another colony was created in Massachusetts by the Puritans. These colonists brought with them their English culture, traditions, religion, and their language. English became the dominant language of the colonies and subsequently of the new nation that was to be formed from the colonies. As the Puritans sought to educate their children, they used the King James Bible, with its rich Latinate vocabulary. In this way, the Greek and Latin roots of English vocabulary spread to North America and took permanent hold.

Beyond these original colonies, the English people and their language have circled the globe. "The sun never sets on the British Empire" was the motto at the time. English is spoken and read around the globe by millions of people. It has influenced the development and history of nations around the world. It has also had an impact on many other languages. However, in the same way that English has influenced other people, lands, and languages, it has also been influenced itself by the people, lands, and languages it has touched. There is hardly a country or culture in the world today that has not had an impact on the English language.

English was influenced by the American Indians living in the Americas during the time of English colonization. Words such as *hickory, moose, skunk,* and *tobacco* are English words that owe their origins to the American Indians who inhabited North America during this period of colonization. Many place names on the North American continent, such as Massachusetts, Ohio, Illinois, Chicago, Omaha, Mississippi, and Dakota, come from the original North Americans. From the Caribbean, discovered by New World explorers, words such as *hammock* and *hurricane* have entered English. From Africa, English has absorbed *yam, banana,* and *canary.* Australia, too, was at one time a colony of England. This is why English is the official language of Australia. As in North America, English was influenced by the language spoken by the native peoples living on the Australian continent at the time of colonization. Words such as *boomerang* and *kangaroo* come from the native Australians and later became adopted as English words.

Conclusion: Learning English Today— The Lessons of History

The English language has a complex and fascinating history. Little wonder, then, that the study of English words is an enriching experience for all of our students. The modern English we speak and write today is the result of the influences and blending of many other languages that touched and even dominated England. To this day, new words are being added or assimilated into English from other languages and cultures that English-speaking people have encountered. The assimilative nature of English has resulted in a rich and complex language—one that is filled with new words ready to express both complex and subtle ideas. However, this richness and complexity can also make English a challenging language to pronounce, spell, and define.

Although English bears the impact of every language it has encountered, it is especially indebted to Greek and Latin for the richness of its vocabulary. As this brief survey has made clear, the indebtedness of English to Latin dates back to the first century B.C. when Julius Caesar crossed the Alps, entered ancient Gaul, and crossed over into Britain. With their troops, the Romans brought Latin into Europe and England, and they also brought the translated culture of the ancient Greeks, whom they admired and respected for their achievements in the letters, sciences, and arts. This culture became even more pronounced during the Renaissance when Europeans rediscovered the ancient Greeks and enriched their vocabularies with words taken directly from Greek, without relying on Latin translators. All this time, church education was rooted in the spiritual and academic vocabulary of the Greek Bible and its subsequent translation into Latin. This tradition continued with the King James Bible, which brought a veritable flood of Latin words into English. To this day, all serious students of English and all students intent on mastering the many content areas of a school curriculum find themselves returning to the ancients and their languages. Far from "dead," Greek and Latin continue to infuse and revitalize an ever-evolving language.

At the outset of this chapter, we commented on the daunting task that teachers face in covering such an enormous word system. But as we review the history of this language and understand how systematic it has been in incorporating Greek- and Latin-based words, we may see a glimmer of light. With a systematic approach to these Greek and Latin word elements, we can begin to sort through the confusing array of word lists and face our teaching mission with excitement and confidence. This book is dedicated to helping teachers and students make the most of the Latin and Greek origins of English words as they teach and learn our language.

Translation of "The Knight's Tale" (refer to pages 151-152):

Once, as old histories tell us,

There was a duke who was called Theseus;

He was lord and governor of Athens,

And in his time such a conqueror

That there was no one greater under the sun.

(http://www.courses.fas.harvard.edu/~chaucer/teachslf/kt-par1.htm)

Resources for Students

In this section, we provide brief descriptions of several types of resources for your students: general websites, children's books that focus on word play, and children's dictionaries.

Websites for Students

edHelper.com
http://www.edhelper.com
This site has more than just vocabulary. Check out the Table of Contents and click on "Vocabulary." In addition to spelling and vocabulary lessons, you will find many ready-to-implement activities about Greek and Latin roots that students will enjoy.

Explore English Words Derived from Latin-Greek Origins
http://www.wordexplorations.com
Students will enjoy "Words for Our Modern Age: Especially English Words from Greek and Latin Sources."

Learning Vocabulary Fun!
http://www.vocabulary.co.il
There is something here for all ages and skill levels. Students can play the match game and Hangman, or do crossword puzzles, word searches, and jumbles. All the activities are for one player.

The Lex Files
http://www.lexfiles.info
Students will enjoy exploring this site of Latin and Greek prefixes, suffixes, and root words. It includes lists of quotations, legal terms, medical words, prescription terms, religious expressions, and various abbreviations from Latin and Greek.

Appendix A *(cont.)*

Surfing the Net with Kids

http://www.surfnetkids.com/games

This site contains free kids' games listed by type (e.g., crossword, jigsaw), topic (e.g., science, geography), or theme (e.g., sports, dress-up, holidays). It also has an easy-to-use search tool.

Vocabulary University

http://www.vocabulary.com

This site is full of puzzles and other activities based on Greek and Latin roots. The puzzles change regularly, so students can visit the site frequently without getting bored.

Word Central

http://www.wordcentral.com

Maintained by *Merriam-Webster*, this site has plenty of activities and information for students, as well as resources (including lesson plans) for teachers. You can even build your own dictionary.

Word Games and Puzzles

http://mindfun.com

Calls itself the "Web's best spot for online trivia games, word puzzles, and quizzes!" Students will find word scrambles, trivia, webs, crossword puzzles—even Boggle.

Children's Books for Word Play

Cleary, B. P. 1999. *A mink, a fink, a skating rink: What is a noun?* Minneapolis, MN: Carolrhoda.

Cleary, B. P. 2001. *To root, to toot, to parachute: What is a verb?* Minneapolis, MN: Carolrhoda.

Cleary, B. P. 2004. *Pitch and throw, grasp and know: What is a synonym?* Minneapolis, MN: Carolrhoda.

Cleary, B. P. 2006. *Stop and go, yes and no: What is an antonym?* Minneapolis, MN: Millbrook.

Appendix A *(cont.)*

Frasier, D. 2000. *Miss Alaineus: A vocabulary disaster.* San Diego, CA: Harcourt.

Gwynne, F. 1976. *A chocolate moose for dinner.* New York: Aladdin.

Gwynne, F. 1987, 2006. *The king who rained.* New York: Aladdin.

Parish, P., and H. Parish. *Amelia Bedelia series.* New York: HarperCollins. http://www.harpercollinschildrens.com/ (Choose from dozens of delightful books about the "word-challenged" Amelia.)

Terban, M. 1982. *Eight ate: A feast of homonym riddles.* New York: Clarion.

Terban, M. 1996. *Dictionary of idioms.* New York: Scholastic. (Includes more than 600 popular phrases, sayings, and expressions.)

Children's Dictionaries

Little Explorers English Picture Dictionary
http://www.enchantedlearning.com/Dictionary.html
Click on a letter of the alphabet and your students will find dozens of words that begin with that letter. Each of the 2,472 words has a picture and a definition. Best of all, this site also has picture dictionaries that go from English to Spanish, French, Italian, Portuguese, German, Swedish, Dutch, and Japanese. These dictionaries will captivate all your students and provide extra support to English language learners. (NOTE: Older students may enjoy working with some of the other electronic dictionaries and resources listed in the Teacher Resources section of this chapter.)

Merriam-Webster Children's Dictionary. 2005. New York: DK Publishing. For ages 4–8.

My First Dictionary. 1993. New York: DK Children. For ages 4–8.

Appendix A *(cont.)*

DK Children's Illustrated Dictionary. 1994. New York: DK Children. For ages 4–8.

Scholastic Children's Dictionary. 2002. New York: Scholastic. For ages 4–8.

Resources for Teachers

This section contains resources to enhance your vocabulary instruction: websites for lists of words and roots, websites that allow you to create vocabulary games and puzzles, electronic dictionaries and other resources, and sites that offer lesson plans related to vocabulary.

Websites for Word Roots/Word Lists

Building Vocabulary

http://www.learner.org/jnorth/tm/tips/Tip0023.html

Sponsored by "Journey North," this site has quick and easy classroom vocabulary activities.

Lists of Latin and Greek Roots

http://www.awrsd.org/oak/Library/greek_and_latin_root_words.htm
http://www.factmonster.com/ipka/A0907017.html
http://academic.cuesta.edu/acasupp/as/506.htm

Most Frequently Used Words Lists

http://www.esldesk.com/esl-quizzes/frequently-used-english-words/words.htm

This useful site will take you, in increments of 300, to the 1,000 most frequently used words in the English language.

Word Roots and Prefixes

http://www.virtualsalt.com/roots.htm

This site has lists of roots and words that come from them.

Websites to Make Your Own Word Games

Discovery School's Word Search Puzzlemaker

http://puzzlemaker.discoveryeducation.com/WordSearchSetupForm.asp

This word-search generator gives options for letter use and word type.

Appendix B *(cont.)*

FunBrain Word Turtle
http://www.funbrain.com/detect

You or your students can give "FunBrain" a list of words that it will hide in a puzzle. Students can choose skill level and play alone or with a friend. Students can also play ready-made puzzles based on some favorite children's literature.

Instant Online Crossword Puzzlemaker
http://www.varietygames.com/CW

Make your own crossword puzzle in a flash and then print for your students to enjoy. You can make the puzzles simple or complicated, so this site is good for teachers working at all levels.

Superkids Word Search Puzzle
http://www.superkids.com/aweb/tools/words/search

Make your own printable hidden word puzzles using the SuperKids Word Search Puzzle Creator. (Only available for PCs.)

Word Search
http://www.armoredpenguin.com/wordsearch

You can use the "generator" to create your own word jumbles and puzzles.

Dictionaries and Reference Books/Websites

AllWords.com
http://www.allwords.com

This site has an online dictionary that does a multilingual search, which is very useful for students who are learning English as a second language. "Links for word lovers" will take you to all kinds of resources for information (dictionaries, thesaurus, etymologies) and word play (puns, rhymes, songs, quotations).

AskOxford.com
http://www.askoxford.com

Here is a free online dictionary from the makers of the famous Oxford English Dictionary. The site includes word games and other support materials for spelling, grammar, etymology, and foreign phrases, plus an "Ask the Experts" link where you can find answers to frequently-asked language questions.

Appendix B *(cont.)*

A.Word.A.Day
http://www.wordsmith.org/awad

Have a new word come straight into your email every day! This site also provides a vocabulary word, its definition, pronunciation information with audio clip, etymology, usage example, and quotation.

The Big List
http://www.wordorigins.org

This site explains the origin of more than 400 familiar words and phrases, selected because they are "interesting or because some bit of folklore, sometimes true and sometimes false, is associated with the origin." Dazzle students with your own knowledge, or let them explore for themselves.

Merriam-Webster Online
http://www.m-w.com

This site has an extensive and easy-to-use online dictionary and thesaurus that even provides audio pronunciations. Students will enjoy free word games and can sign up for Word of the Day.

One Look Dictionary Search
http://www.onelook.com

Type in a word and let this site look it up in several dictionaries! It also has a "Reverse Dictionary." Type in a description of the concept and it finds words and phrases that match it.

Online Etymology Dictionary
http://www.wordexplorations.com

Type in any word and this dictionary will tell you its history.

Thesaurus.com
http://thesaurus.reference.com

Type in a word and quickly find synonyms and antonyms for it. This site also has a dictionary, an encyclopedia, and a word of the day in English and Spanish.

American Heritage Dictionaries, eds. 2004. *100 words every high school freshman should know*. Boston: Houghton Mifflin.

Appendix B *(cont.)*

Beeler, D. 1988. *Book of roots: A full study of our families of words.* Chicago: Union Representative.

Funk, C. 2002. *Thereby hangs a tale: Stories of curious word origins.* New York: Collins.

Funk, W. 1992. *Word origins: An exploration and history of words and language.* San Antonio, TX: Wings Books. (Originally published in 1950.) Arranged thematically, this book gives the history and derivation of hundreds of familiar and not-so-familiar words.

Jack, A. 2005. *Red herrings and white elephants: The origins of phrases we use every day.* New York: HarperCollins.

Liberman, A. 2005. *Word origins...and how we know them.* New York: Oxford University Press.

Lesson Plans

Education World
http://www.educationworld.com/a_lesson/lesson/lesson328.shtml
Word Wall activities

LD Resource Room
http://www.resourceroom.net/comprehension/vocabactivities.asp
Although prepared for students with learning disabilities, these activities will benefit general education students as well.

Ohio Resource Center for Math, Science, and Reading
http://ohiorc.org/for/ela/Default.aspx
This address takes you to the English/Language Arts section where you can find hundreds of vocabulary lessons suitable for students of all ages.

Read•Write•Think
http://readwritethink.org
This site, cosponsored by the International Reading Association and the National Council of Teachers of English, contains lesson plans spanning all

Appendix B *(cont.)*

aspects of the language arts and all grade levels as well. To find vocabulary plans, select "Learning about Language" and then "Vocabulary." You can also narrow your search by selecting a grade-level band.

Further Professional Reading
Websites and Online Articles

Elaboration Technique

http://www.ldonline.org/article/5759

This site describes a way to support vocabulary learning among students with learning disabilities.

everythingESL.net

http://www.everythingesl.net/inservices/elementary_sites_ells_
     71638.php

This site provides links to dozens of sites (identified according to grade level) with activities that English language learners will enjoy and benefit from.

A Focus on Vocabulary

http://www.prel.org/products/re_/ES0419.htm

From Pacific Resources for Education and Learning and written by Lehr, Osborn, and Hiebert, this document provides an excellent overview of vocabulary research with in-depth information in a reader-friendly format. This downloadable booklet (44 pages) from the Research-Based Practices in Early Reading series could be used for additional professional development or even shared with parents.

A Little Latin...and a Lot of English

http://ohiorc.org/adlit/ip_content.aspx?recID=159&parentID=158

This article, written by Newton and Newton and available in an online journal sponsored by the Ohio Resource Center for Mathematics, Science, and Reading, offers guidelines and resources for teaching the "classic vocabulary" approach and are woven through a happy school memory of "Roots Day."

Appendix B *(cont.)*

Making and Writing Words

http://www.readingonline.org/articles/art_index.
asp?HREF=words/index.html

Tim Rasinski's popular word-study activity is available at Reading Online, an online journal sponsored by the International Reading Association. You will find detailed planning instructions, classroom examples, blackline masters, and a discussion forum where you can share tips with other teachers.

Reading First—Vocabulary

http://www.nifl.gov/partnershipforreading/publications/reading_
first1vocab.html

Sections of this report include "Vocabulary Instruction," "Types of Vocabulary," "Direct and Indirect Learning" (which includes vocabulary learning), and "An Example of Classroom Instruction."

Reading—Vocabulary

http://www.literacymatters.org/content/readandwrite/vocab.htm

This site includes links to lesson plans for content vocabulary, "tools" for teaching vocabulary, strategy descriptions, and general vocabulary activities.

Vocabulary Acquisition: Synthesis of the Research
http://idea.uoregon.edu/~ncite/documents.html

Baker, Simmons, and Kameenui offer a research-based analysis of the diversity of word learning styles. The document, funded by the U.S. Office of Special Education Programs, can be found at the National Center to Improve the Tools of Educators website. Look for it under "Technical Reports of Reading Research Syntheses."

Vocabulary Learning Online

http://www.readingonline.org/newliteracies/lit_index.
asp?HREF=webwatch/vocabulary/index.html

If you are interested in more ideas about how students can use the Web for vocabulary growth, read Karen Bromley's article in Reading Online.

Appendix B *(cont.)*

Visualizing Vocabulary

http://www.nwp.org/cs/public/print/resource/quarterly/
    Q2002no3/simmons.html

This article comes from the National Writing Project website. It describes
several activities that foster word learning and practice through illustrations.

Teacher Resource Books and Articles

Allen, J. 1999. *Words, words, words: Teaching vocabulary in
    grades 4–12*. Portland, MA: Stenhouse. A fourth-grade
    teacher shares dozens of wonderful and easy-to-implement
    strategies ready for duplicating.

Beck, I. L., M. G. McKeown, and L. Kucan. 2002. *Bringing
    words to life: Robust vocabulary instruction*. New York:
    Guilford. Explains a three-tier system for choosing and
    teaching vocabulary for reading comprehension.

Blachowicz, C., and P. J. Fisher. 2006. *Teaching vocabulary in
    all classrooms*. 3rd ed. Upper Saddle River, NJ: Merrill/
    Prentice-Hall. Each chapter is full of classroom-tested
    strategies. Topics include content-area vocabulary,
    integrating reading and writing, learning from context,
    using reference sources, word play, and assessment.

Brand, M. 2004. *Word savvy: Integrated vocabulary, spelling,
    and word study, grades 3–6*. Portland, MA: Stenhouse. A
    fifth-grade teacher describes how he weaves word study
    throughout the day. Provides advice and many specific
    examples that are easily adaptable to the primary grades.

Brassell, D., and J. Flood. 2004. *Vocabulary strategies every
    teacher needs to know*. San Diego, CA: Academic
    Professional Development. Twenty-five strategies, some
    familiar and some new, with easy-to-follow instructions
    and easy-to-duplicate templates.

Appendix B *(cont.)*

Bromley, K. 2007. Nine things every teacher should know about words and vocabulary instruction. *Journal of Adolescent and Adult Literacy* 50 (7): 528–39.

Bromley, K. 2007. *Stretching students' vocabulary*. New York: Scholastic.

Carris, J. D. 1994. *Success with words*. Princeton, NJ: Peterson's Guides. This workbook has hundreds of root words and "context" activities based on vocabulary needed for success on the SAT and similar standardized tests. The activities are fun to do, and the explanations are very clear. (These are better for older students.)

Fitzgerald, J., and M. Graves. 2004. *Scaffolding reading experiences for English-language learners*. Norwood, MA: Christopher Gordon. The focus of this text is on teaching reading to second-language learners; it includes excellent suggestions for how to introduce these students to new vocabulary.

Fry, E. B. 2004. *The vocabulary teacher's book of lists*. San Francisco, CA: Jossey-Bass. Lists of words from content areas like math and science to word study with prefixes, roots, and homophones.

Garg, A., and S. Garg. 2003. *A word a day: A romp through some of the most unusual and intriguing words in English*. Hoboken, NJ: John Wiley & Sons. Sections include "Animal Words," "Latin Terms," "Words to Describe People," "Lesser-Known Counterparts of Everyday Words," and more.

Kamola, L., ed. 2008. *Successful strategies for reading in the content areas* series. 2nd ed. Huntington Beach, CA: Shell Education. Each book in this series has a detailed chapter about teaching vocabulary development strategies using nonfiction text. Many strategies are given, and graphic organizers are provided when appropriate.

Appendix B *(cont.)*

Macceca, S. 2007. *Reading strategies for science*. Huntington Beach, CA: Shell Education. Learn practical standards-based strategies for teaching vocabulary in science. Each strategy includes specific instructions for differentiating instruction for English language learners, gifted students, and struggling students.

Macceca, S. 2007. *Reading strategies for social studies*. Huntington Beach, CA: Shell Education. Learn practical standards-based strategies for teaching vocabulary in social studies. Each strategy includes specific instructions for differentiating instruction for English language learners, gifted students, and struggling students.

Macceca, S., and T. Brummer. 2008. *Reading strategies for Mathematics*. Huntington Beach, CA: Shell Education. Learn practical standards-based strategies for teaching vocabulary in mathematics. Each strategy includes specific instructions for differentiating instruction for English language learners, gifted students, and struggling students.

Nagy, W. E. 1988. *Teaching vocabulary to improve reading comprehension*. Urbana, IL: National Council of Teachers of English. Short, readable "classic" in vocabulary instruction. Explains the "why" and "how to" of effective instruction for middle school and beyond.

Paynter, D., E. Bodrova, and J. K. Doty. 2005. *For the love of words: Vocabulary instruction that works*. San Francisco, CA: Jossey-Bass. Practical ideas for expanding the role of vocabulary in reading, writing, and thinking.

Rasinski, T. 2005. *Daily word ladders (grades 2–3)*. New York: Scholastic. Students will enjoy the challenge of "climbing" these 100 developmentally appropriate (and easily duplicated) word ladders.

Appendix B *(cont.)*

Rasinski, T. 2005. *Daily word ladders (grades 4–6)*. New York: Scholastic. Provides 100 reproducible "ladders" for students to enjoy "climbing" as they use vocabulary practice to enhance critical thinking.

Rasinski, T., and R. Heym. *Making and writing words (grades 2–3)*. Huntington Beach, CA: Shell Education. Over 40 ready-to-use word activities that help students improve their phonemic awareness, phonics, spelling, and vocabulary skills.

Rasinski, T., and N. Padak. 2004. *Effective reading strategies: Teaching children who find reading difficult*. 3rd ed. Columbus, OH: Merrill/Prentice Hall. Identifies strategies that target specific needs, including vocabulary and word study, of students who can use extra support in learning to read.

Rasinski, T., N. Padak, R. Newton, and E. Newton. 2006. *Building vocabulary from word roots (levels 3–8)*. Huntington Beach, CA: Teacher Created Materials (Beach City Press). Introduces a new root each week, with daily guided practice activities. (Set includes teacher's manual with transparencies and full-color workbooks for students.)

Stahl, S. 1999. *Vocabulary development*. Cambridge, MA: Brookline. An excellent review of what we know about vocabulary learning and what sort of instruction supports vocabulary development.

Commonly Taught Roots

The following roots chart will assist you in your vocabulary instruction. The first column provides a list of commonly taught Latin and Greek roots (including bases, prefixes, and suffixes); the second column provides the meaning of each root; and the third column provides sample words that utilize each root. The column of sample words is intended to give you a sense how the roots are used—it is by no means an exhaustive selection. These sample words are best used as a starting point for further developing your vocabulary instruction; as students gain more proficiency with roots and root meanings, they will begin to come up with words on their own.

Bases	Meaning	Sample Words
(a)llel	one another	parallel
(h)od	road	odometer, cathode
(s)ent, essent, essence	be	absent, present, essential
ag, act, igu	drive, go	agile, action, ambiguous
adelph	brother	Philadelphia
aer(o)	air, wind	aerate
agog(ue), agogy	lead	pedagogy, synagogue
al, alma	nourishing	alimony, alma mater
alg	pain, ache	nostalgic
am(a), amat, amor	love, friend	amiable, amateur, amorous
ambul	walk	ambulatory
angel	messenger	angelic
angle	angle	quadrangle

Appendix C *(cont.)*

Bases	Meaning	Sample Words
anim	life, soul	animated
annu, enni	year	annual, perennial
anthrop(o)	human being, mankind	anthropology
ap(i)	bee	apiary
aqu, aqua	water	aqueduct, aquatic
aquil	eagle	aquiline
astr(o)	star	astrology
athl	contest, struggle	athletics
audi, audit	hear, listen	audience, audition
avi	bird	aviator
barbar	savage(ry)	barbarous
bell(i), bellum	war	bellicose, ante bellum
bi(o)	live, life	biology
bibli(o)	book	bibliophile
bol	throw	symbol
bon, bene	good, well	bonanza, benevolent
bov	cow	bovine
brev	short	abbreviate
bys(s)	bottom	abyss, abysmal
can	dog	canine
cap, capt, cept, ceive	take, seize, get	captivity, receive, perception
caps	case	capsule
cardi	heart	cardiac
ced, ceed, cess	go, move, yield	recede, proceed, excess
celer	swift	accelerate

Appendix C *(cont.)*

Bases	Meaning	Sample Words
cent	one hundred	century
center, centr	center	eccentric
chrom	color	chromatic
chron(o)	time	chronic
cid, cis	cut, kill	genocide, excise
clam, clamat, claim	shout	proclamation, exclamatory, acclaim
class	classic	neoclassic
clin	lie, lean	recline
clud, clus, clos	close, shut	exclude, inclusion, enclose
col	strain, sieve	percolate
corn(u)	horn	cornucopia
cosm(o)	world, order	cosmonaut, cosmetic
cotta	cooked, baked	terra cotta
cred, credit	believe	incredible, accredited
cub, cumb	lie, lean	incubate, incumbent
cur, curs, cour, cours	run, go	concur, cursive, courier, concourse
cuss	hit, strike	percussion
cycl(e)	wheel	unicycle
dec, decim, decem	ten	decimal, December
dei, divin	god	deify, divinity
dem	the people	epidemic
dent	tooth, teeth	dentures
derm, dermat	skin	hypodermic, dermatitis

Appendix C *(cont.)*

Bases	Meaning	Sample Words
dexter, dextr	right hand	dexterity, ambidextrous
dic, dict	say, speak, tell	predict
dos(e), dot(e)	give	dosage, antidote
duc, duct	lead	induce, deduct
dynam	power, strength, strong	dynamic
ec(o)	environment, house	ecology
elephan	elephant	elephantine
enni, annu	year	biennial, biannual
erg	work	ergonomic
fac, fic, fact, fect, feit, fit	do, make	facilities, factory, benefit
fal, fall, fals, fail, fault	false, mistake, fail	falsify, fallible, default
fel	cat	feline
fend, fens	strike	offend, defensive
fer, lat	to bear, bring, go	confer, collate
fess	speak	confess
fin, finit	end, limit, term	final, finite
flat	air, blow	inflate
flect, flex	bend	deflect, reflex
foc	focus	focal
for	hole, opening, doorway	perforated
forc, fort	power, strength, strong	enforce, fortify
form	form, shape	formal

Appendix C *(cont.)*

Bases	Meaning	Sample Words
found, fund, fus	pour, melt	foundry, refund, confuse
fum	smoke, vapor	fumigate
funct	perform	function
gam	marriage	polygamist
ge(o)	earth	geometry
gen, gener	be born, give birth, produce	genius, generation
ger, geront	elderly	geriatric, gerontology
glob	globe, sphere	globular
gnos, gnost	read, know	diagnosis, agnostic
grad, gress	step, go	gradual, congress
graph, gram	write, draw	graphite, telegram
greg	flock, herd	gregarious, congregate
gyn, gynec	woman	gynecology
habit	dwell, keep	inhabit
hal(e)	breathe	inhale, halitosis
haute	high	Terre Haute
(h)em, hemat	blood	anemia, hematology
hemer	day	ephemeral
hemi	one half	hemisphere
hepta	seven	heptagon
her, hes	stick, cling	coherent, adhesive
hexa	six	hexagon
hor(o)	hour	horoscope
horr	frighten	horrify

Appendix C *(cont.)*

Bases	Meaning	Sample Words
hum	damp earth	humus, humidity
human	human being, mankind	humane
hydr(o)	water	hydrant
hypno	sleep	hypnosis
i, it	go	exit, transient
iatr	doctor	pediatrician
ig(u), ag, act	drive, go	ambiguous, agile, action
jac, ject	throw	eject
jur, juris	judge, oath	jury, jurisdiction
kilo	one thousand	kilogram
lab	take	syllable
labor	work	laborious
later	side	unilateral
lav	wash	lavatory
leg, lig, lect	pick, read	legible, eligible, collect
leo(n)	lion	leonine
libr	book	librarian
lingu	language	linguistics
liter	letter	literature, illiterate
lith	stone	monolith
loc, locat	place	local, location
locut, loqu	speak, talk	elocution, eloquent
log	word, reason, study	logic
luc, lumin	light	lucid, luminous

Appendix C *(cont.)*

Bases	Meaning	Sample Words
lud, lus	play, trick, mock	elude, illusion
lup	wolf	lupine
m(eridiem)	noon, midday	ante meridiem (A.M.)
magn	big	magnify
mal(e)	bad, wrong	malevolent, malign
man, main	stay, remain	permanent, remain
man(u)	hand	manual
mast	round bump, protrusion	mastoid
matr(i), matern	mother	matrimony, maternal
me(a)	wander, go	meander
medi	middle	medium
meter, metr(o), metr(i)	measure	centimeter, metronome, metric
mill	one thousand	millimeter
miss, mit	send	missile, permit
mnem, mnes	memory	mnemonic, amnesia
mole	mass	molecule
mon(o)	alone, only, one	monologue
mord, mors	bite	mordant, morsel
morph	shape, form	amorphous
mor, mort	dead	moribund, mortal
mov, mot, mobil	move	move, promote, mobile
mur	wall	mural
nat, natur, nasc	be born, give birth, produce	prenatal, natural, nascent

Appendix C *(cont.)*

Bases	Meaning	Sample Words
navig	sail	navigate
neo	new	neonatal
nihil	nothing	annihilate
noc, nox	harm	innocent, noxious
nomin	name	nominate
non, nov	nine	nonagon, November
noun	name	pronoun
nov	new	innovate
oct(a)	eight	octave
ocl(e), ocul	eye	monocle, binoculars
od	song	parody, ode
odont	tooth, teeth	periodontics
omni	all, every	omnipotent
onym	word, name	pseudonym
orth(o)	straight	orthodonture
ov	sheep	ovine
pac	peace	pacify
pan, pan(t)	all, every	panacea, pantomime
par, pear	appearance, seem	apparition, disappear
par, part	produce, beget	separate, post partum
past, pastor	shepherd	pasture, pastoral
path(o)	feel(ing), suffer(ing)	sympathy, pathology
pati, pass	feel(ing), suffer(ing)	patient, compassion
patr(i), patern	father, fatherland	patriot, paternity
ped	foot, feet	pedal, impede
pel, puls, peal	drive, push	dispel, impulse, repeal

Appendix C *(cont.)*

Bases	Meaning	Sample Words
pend, pens	weigh, hang, pay	pendant, suspense
penta	five	pentagon
petr	stone	petrify
phem	word, saying	euphemism
pher	bear, go	periphery
phil(o), phil(e)	love, friend	philodendron, Anglophile
phon	voice, call, sound	telephone
photo	light	photograph
phragm	block, enclose	diaphragm
phyt	plant	neophyte
plac	calm, please	placate
ple, plex, ply	fold, multiply	multiple, duplex, imply
plur, plus	more	plural, plus
pne, pneum	breathe	apnea, pneumonia
pol, polis, polit	city, citizen	acropolis, political
pon, pos, posit, pound	put, place	components, positive, compound
port	carry	import
poss, pot	power	impossible, potentate
preci	price, value	precious
punct(u), pung	pierce	puncture, pungent
quadr, quart	four	quadrant, quarter
quint	five	quintuplets
ras	scrape	rash, erase
reg, rig, rect	straight, guide	regular, incorrigible, correct

Appendix C *(cont.)*

Bases	Meaning	Sample Words
rupt	break	interrupt
sanct(u)	holy, sacred	sanctuary
scend, scens	step, climb	descend, ascension
scop	look, watch	microscope
scrib, script	write	scribe, scripture
sec, sect	cut, slice	secant, section
secut, sequ	follow	prosecute, sequel
sed, sid, sess	sit, settle	sediment, reside, session
semi	one half	semicircle
sent, sens	think, feel	sentence, sensation
seps, sept	infection	sepsis, antiseptic
sept(em), sept(a)	seven	septet, September
serv, servat	save, keep, serve	servile, reservation
sex	six	sextet
sist	stand	persist
sit	food, feed	parasite
sol(i)	alone, only, one	soliloquy
solv, solut	free, loosen	dissolve, solution
somn(i)	sleep	somnambulist, somniloquist
son, sound	sound	resonate, resound
soph	wisdom, wise	philosophy
sorb	soak	absorb
spec, spic, spect	watch, look at	specimen, conspicuous, spectacle

Appendix C *(cont.)*

Bases	Meaning	Sample Words
spir, (s)pir	breathe	perspire, expire
sta, stanc, stat	stand	stable, circumstance, static
stle, stol	send	epistle, apostolic
strain, strict, string	tie, bind, squeeze	restrain, restrict, stringent
stru, struct	build	construe, destructive
sui (swi)	pig, hog	swine
tang, ting, tig, tact	touch	tangent, contingent, contiguous, intact
taph	grave, tomb	epitaph
taur	bull	Minotaur
techn	art, skill, fine craft	technique
tempor	time	temporary
ten, tin, tent, tain	hold	tenacious, continent, contents, retain
tend, tens, tenu	stretch, thin	extend, tensile, tenuous
terr, ter	land, ground, earth	inter, territory
test	witness	testify
tetra	four	tetrahedron
thanas, thanat	death	euthanasia
theater, theatr	theater, watch	theatrical
the(o)	god	atheist, theology
therm	heat	thermal
thes, thet	put, place	thesis, synthetic
tom	cut	anatomy

Appendix C *(cont.)*

Bases	Meaning	Sample Words
ton	tone	monotonous
trac, tract, treat	pull, draw, drag	trace, tractor, retreat
trop	turn	tropics
trud, trus	push, thrust	intrude, protrusion
turb	shake, agitate	turbulence
urs	bear (the animal)	ursine, Ursa Major
val	be strong, be healthy	valid
ven, vent	come	convene, advent
ventr(i)	belly	ventriloquist
ver	true	veritable
verb	word	verbal
vers, vert	turn, change	adverse, advertise
vest	clothing	vestments
via	way, road	viaduct
vid, vis	see	video, visual
vigil	awake	vigilant
vit, viv	live, life	vital, revive
voc, voke, voice	voice, call, sound	vocal, revoke, invoice
vol	wish, will	volunteer
volv, volu, volut	roll	revolve, volume, revolution
vor	eat, devour	voracious
vulp	fox	vulpine
zo(o)	animal	zodiac, zoology

Appendix C *(cont.)*

Prefixes	Meaning	Sample Words
a, ab, abs	away, from	avert, abduct, abstain
a, an	not, without	atheist, anemia
ad (+assimilated forms)	to, toward, add to	addition, aggregate, attract
ambi	around, on both sides	ambidextrous
amphi	around, on both sides	amphibian
ana	back, again, apart	analyze
ante	before	antecedent
anti, ant	against, opposite	antithesis, antonym
auto	self	autocrat, automobile
bi	two	bicycle
circu, circum	around	circuit, circumference
co, con (+ assimilated forms)	with, together, very	cohesion, connect, compose, collection, correct
contra, contro, counter	against, opposite	contradict, controversy, counterpoint
de	down, off of	demotion, descent
di, dis, dif	apart, in different directions, not	divert, dismiss, differ
dia	through, across, thorough	diameter
dys	bad, improper	dysfunction
e, ef, ex	out, out of, very	emit, effective, exceed
em, en	in, on	emblem, encircle
epi	upon, to, in addition to	epidermis
eu, ev	good, well	eulogy, evangelist
hypo	below, under, up from under	hypothermia

Appendix C *(cont.)*

Prefixes	Meaning	Sample Words
in, im, il	not (negative)	inequity, improper, illegal
in, im, il	in, on, into (directional)	induct, impose, illuminate
infra	beneath	infrastructure
inter	between, among	intervene
mega, megalo	big	megachurch, megalomaniac
meta	across, change	metamorphosis
micro	small	microcosm
mis	wrongly	misinterpret, mistake
multi	many	multivitamin
ob (+ assimilated forms)	up against, in the way	obstruct, oppose, offend
para	aside, apart	paramedic, paranormal
per	through, thorough, wrongly	permeate, persecute
peri	around	perimeter
poly	many	polytheism
post	after	postpone
pre	before	precedent
pro	forward, ahead, for	promotion, provoke
re	back, again	repel, revise
se	aside, apart	secession
sub (+assimilated forms)	below, under, up from under	submarine, suffer, suppose
super, sur	on top of, over, above	supersede, surreal
syn, sym, syl	with, together	synthesis, symphony, syllogism
tele	far, from afar	telegram

Appendix C *(cont.)*

Prefixes	Meaning	Sample Words
trans, tra	across, change	transpose, travesty
tri	three	trinity
un	not	unruly
uni, unit	one	unique, unite

Suffixes	Meaning	Sample Words
(l)et, (i)cle, (ic)ule	small	booklet, icicle, molecule
(o)logy	word, reason, study of	biology
able, ible	can or able to be done	portable, audible
ance, ancy, ence, ency	the state or quality of	importance, hesitancy, patience, fluency
ant, ent	having the quality of	flagrant, potent
arch	rule	monarch
arium, ary, orium, ory	place, room	aquarium, library, auditorium, laboratory
(as)tery, (e)tery	place	monastery, cemetery
ate	to make or do	equate
ation	the result of making or doing	incarnation
cracy	rule by	plutocracy
crat	ruler, one who believes in rule by	democrat
ectomy	surgical removal, "cutting out"	tonsillectomy
el, il, le	small	morsel, codicil, scruple
ella	small	umbrella
er	more	faster, bigger

Appendix C *(cont.)*

Suffixes	Meaning	Sample Words
er, or	someone who does, something that does	teacher, instructor
est	most	noblest, smartest
ful	full of	bountiful, plentiful
ify	to make	beautify
ist	one who does	artist
less	without	tireless
ly	in a _____ way or manner	slowly
ologist	studier of, expert in	hematologist
ose, ous, eous, ious	full of	verbose, populous, aqueous, spacious
phobe	one who fears	acrophobe
phobia	fear of	claustrophobia

Beyond Latin and Greek

The English language has certainly been influenced greatly by Latin and Greek. To this day, Latin and Greek continue to play a role in the introduction of new words into English, especially the new words that come from science and technology. Scientists and scholars will often lean on Latin and Greek when coming up with new words to express novel concepts and discoveries.

However, Latin and Greek are not the only languages that have had an impact on English. In our chapter on the history of English, we noted that whenever England was invaded by another group, the language of the new group had a significant influence on English. From the original Germanic invaders to the Vikings and the French, English has taken on words and characteristics of those people and their cultures.

The story of English would not be complete without an acknowledgement that English has been influenced by nearly every land, language, and culture that it has come into contact with. The following is a sampling of these words of influence.

African		
aardvark	impala	voodoo
bango	jazz	yarn
bongo	safari	zebra
gumbo	trek	zombie

American Indian		
caribou	hickory	opossum
chili	kayak	powwow
chocolate	moccasin	skunk
cougar	moose	squash
Eskimo	muskrat	tomahawk

Appendix D *(cont.)*

Arabic		
alcohol	bungalow	jasmine
algebra	camphor	giraffe
apricot	chemistry	sofa
arsenal	cotton	tariff
artichoke	crimson	zenith
atlas	hazard	zero

Australian (Aboriginal)		
dingo	koala	wombat
kangaroo	wallaby	yabber

Chinese		
chow	ketchup	tea
ginseng	kowtow	wok
gingko	kung fu	
gung ho	sampan	

French		
accommodation	hospital	scholar
accomplish	jacket	surgeon
celebrate	porpoise	unique
female	rebound	vigorous
foliage	resume	villain
genius	savant	
gracious	restaurant	

German		
blitz	gestalt	pretzel
bratwurst	hinterland	sauerkraut
delicatessen	kindergarten	wanderlust
ersatz	poltergeist	zeitgeist

Appendix D *(cont.)*

Hebrew		
amen	rabbi	Satan
hallelujah	jubilee	schwa
kibbutz	Sabbath	

Indian		
anaconda	ginger	nirvana
bangle	guru	orange
caravan	juggernaut	pundit
cot	loot	sandal
emerald	mantra	sentry

Irish		
bard	dork	razz
bicker	giggle	scalawag
bother	guzzle	shindig
cantankerous	hoax	sneeze
cold turkey	pet	taunt
dude	phony	

Italian		
bank	mandolin	porcelain
bulletin	medal	rotunda
buffoon	model	soda
coffee	paparazzi	solo
graffiti	pizza	virtue

Japanese		
futon	hooch	samurai
haiku	judo	soy
hibachi	karaoke	sushi
honcho	ninja	tycoon

Appendix D *(cont.)*

Scandinavian (Old Norse, Danish, Norwegian, Swedish)		
birth	ombudsmen	slalom
blunder	ransack	tungsten
fjord	saga	wand
flounder	skin	wicker
guest	skirt	window
oaf	sky	ugly

Scottish		
bog	glen	slob
caddy	golf	slogan
clan	plaid	smidgen
galore	rampage	trousers
glamour	slew	whisky

Spanish		
adios	embargo	silo
bonanza	guerilla	tomato
cafeteria	mustang	tortilla
corral	patio	vamoose
coyote	renegade	vanilla

Slavic (including Czech, Polish, Russian, Slovak)		
babushka	intelligentsia	robot
bistro	kasha	ruble
dacha	kielbasa	steppe
gulag	pogrom	sable
howitzer	polka	vodka

Yiddish		
bagel	klutz	schmooze
blintz	kosher	shtick
glitch	nosh	

Professional Development Ideas

Each chapter in this book explores a different dimension of vocabulary study based on Latin and Greek roots. Many of the ideas in these chapters can be adapted to your own classroom needs. You can use the following questions and suggestions for personal reflection and professional conversation with colleagues:

1. Think back to the vocabulary instruction that characterized your own school years. What were you asked to do with words? Try to identify at least three activities that stand out. How effective were they? Did they lead to word learning?

   Share your memories with each other by comparing the activities and their effectiveness. Are there any similarities? If so, can you make any generalizations about vocabulary learning in American classrooms?

2. If you could make three changes to your vocabulary program, what would they be? Select the most important change and make an action plan for achieving it.

   Share your plans with each other. Give each other feedback. Make sure to jot down any suggestions that seem particularly good.

3. If you or your colleagues are currently using a vocabulary program, evaluate it. Identify its strengths and weaknesses. The following questions (adapted from Newton et al. 2008) may assist you as you analyze and discuss your findings:

Appendix E *(cont.)*

- What is the logic inherent in the words selected for focus? Are the words appropriate for your students' developmental levels?

- Do your students find the activities engaging?

- Do the activities help your students build and deepen their conceptual knowledge?

- Do students learn and apply word analysis strategies, particularly the study of word roots and context clues?

- Do activities feature student discussion about vocabulary?

- Are there opportunities for metacognitive growth?

- Are whole-group, small-group, and individual activities plentiful and appropriate?

- Do activities promote interest in words? Are activities gamelike and playful?

- Does the program offer strategies to differentiate instruction so that all learners can grow?

- Are a variety of scaffolding practices available for students who need it?

- Is the amount of time per day appropriate (10–15 minutes daily)?

- Is the overall instructional routine appropriate?

- Does the program fit well with the rest of your literacy curriculum?

- Are assessment ideas offered?

Appendix E *(cont.)*

4. Identify a student whose vocabulary is particularly good. Think about why he or she stands out and make a list of observable indicators. Now identify a student whose vocabulary is limited. Make a second list of his or her observable indicators.

    Share your lists with each other. Are there similarities among the indicators you have listed? If so, discuss how you might use some of the ideas in this book to differentiate instruction for students with advanced or limited vocabularies.

5. What key math, social studies, and science concepts are you responsible for teaching? Make a list of key vocabulary words in each area. Identify five to ten of the most common prefixes and bases in those words. Develop an action plan for teaching those roots.

    Share your list of roots and your action plan with colleagues. Give each other feedback. Make sure to jot down any suggestions that seem particularly good.

6. Even though their English language skills are often limited, students who speak a language other than English can enhance the vocabulary learning experience of all students. Think about the English language learners in your classroom. What first languages do they speak? What cultural backgrounds do they represent? What unique contributions can they make to vocabulary and root study?

    Share your ideas with colleagues. Discuss how your English language learners' linguistic and cultural strengths might be used to highlight some of the ideas in this book.

7. Chapter 5 presents several classroom-tested "practice activities" to support vocabulary development. Identify two or three of those activities that are especially well suited to your students. Make concrete plans to implement each one by considering why, when, and how you will use it.

Appendix E *(cont.)*

Share the activities and plans with your colleagues. Give each other feedback. Make sure to jot down any suggestions that seem particularly good.

8. In Chapter 6, you read an excerpt from "A Little Latin…and a Lot of English" (Newton and Newton 2005) in which Rick Newton fondly recalls "Roots Day" in his ninth grade Latin class. Go to the Ohio Resource Center's e-journal, "Adolescent Literacy in Perspective" and read the entire article. (http://www.ohiorc.org/adlit/, Click on "Browse Archives" by author to locate the article.)

Now select one of the following guidelines from the article as an area of focus, and brainstorm new activities you might implement to enhance your vocabulary program in this area:

- Tuck "word talk" into all lessons.
- Encourage students to become word sleuths.
- Teach the word-analysis strategy of Divide and Conquer.
- Provide direct instruction for key vocabulary.
- Share your own love of words with your students.
- Make time for word play.
- Promote wide reading on a variety of topics.

Share your ideas with each other. Give each other feedback. Make sure to jot down any suggestions that seem particularly good. (You may be interested in using a professional development module built around this article for additional vocabulary study with your colleagues. Go to http://www.ohiorc.org/adlit, click on "Professional Development Modules" and then "Vocabulary.")

Appendix E *(cont.)*

9. Chapter 8 encourages an expanded role for dictionaries in the vocabulary classroom. Reflect on your current use of dictionaries. Do you have several different types? How recent are they? Do they represent a range of reading levels?

   How do you use them in classroom instruction? Now think about how you might use some of the ideas in this chapter to expand the role of dictionaries in your classroom.

   Share your ideas with each other. Jot down those ideas that seem particularly well suited to your classroom needs.

10. Appendices A and B provide electronic and print resources for you and for your students. Review the resources and choose one student resource and one teacher resource that you think may be particularly useful.

    Explore those resources and report your findings to colleagues. Describe the content and explain how you might use them. Note any resources they report on that seem well suited to your instructional needs.

#50472—Greek and Latin Roots © Shell Education

Glossary

active vocabulary—the words we know well enough to use in speaking or writing

affix—a morpheme that changes the meaning or function of a root to which it is attached

assimilate—to make a sound similar to or identical to an adjacent sound in order to ease pronunciation

base—a word or word part to which affixes may be added to create related words. Also called a root or base word.

cognate—a word related in form and meaning to another word. This relationship is the result of the words sharing a common source.

colloquial/colloquialism—informal or spoken language

compound word—a combination of two or more words that functions as a single unit

context—the "linguistic environment" (Harris and Hodges 1995, 44); the words or phrases adjacent to another language unit

decontextualized—having the context taken away

derivative—a word formed by adding an affix; a related word

figurative language—language containing images and other nonliteral language

lingua franca—a common language used by diverse cultures in shared communication

metacognition—an awareness and knowledge of one's thought processes. Applied to reading, this ordinarily refers to

Glossary *(cont.)*

the reader's ability to monitor reading and apply fix-up strategies should they be necessary.

metalinguistics—an awareness and knowledge of language as an object itself

metaphor—a type of figurative language in which a comparison is implied but not directly stated

morpheme—the smallest unit of language that carries meaning

morphology—the study of the forms and structure of words

neologism—a new word

passive vocabulary—the words we understand in reading or in listening

phoneme—the smallest unit of language that carries sound

polysemy—words that have more than one meaning

prefix—an affix attached before a base word

romance languages—"any of the Italic Indo-European languages derived from Latin in the Middle Ages; chiefly French, Spanish, Italian, Portuguese, and Romanian" (Harris and Hodges 1995, 222)

root—"the basic part of a word that usually carries the main component of meaning and that cannot be further identified without loss of identity" (Harris and Hodges 1995, 222)

semantic context—the meaning of words or phrases adjacent to another language unit

suffix—an affix attached after a base word

syntactic context—the word order (grammar) of words or phrases adjacent to another language unit

References Cited

Ayers, D. M. 1986. *English words from Latin and Greek elements*. Tucson, AZ: University of Arizona Press.

Banks, K. 2006. *Max's words*. New York: Farrar, Straus, and Giroux.

Baumann, J. F., G. Font, E. C. Edwards, and E. Boland. 2005. Strategies for teaching middle-grade students to use word-part and context clues to expand reading vocabulary. In *Teaching and learning vocabulary*, ed. E. Hiebert and M. Kamil, 179–205. Mahwah, NJ: Erlbaum.

Baumann, J., E. Kameenui, and G. Ash. 2003. Research on vocabulary instruction: Voltaire redux. In *Handbook of research on teaching the English language arts*. 2nd ed. Ed. J. Flood, D. Lapp, J. Squire, and J. Jensen, 752–85. Hillsdale, NJ: Erlbaum.

Bear, D., M. Invernizzi, S. Templeton, and F. Johnston. 2000. *Words their way*. 2nd ed. Upper Saddle River, NJ: Prentice Hall.

Biemiller, A. 2005. Size and sequence in vocabulary development: Implications for choosing words for primary grade vocabulary instruction. In *Teaching and learning vocabulary*, ed. E. Hiebert and M. Kamil, 223–42. Mahwah, NJ: Erlbaum.

Blachowicz, C., and P. Fisher. 2002. *Teaching vocabulary in all classrooms*. 2nd ed. Upper Saddle River, NJ: Merrill/ Prentice Hall.

———. 2006. *Teaching vocabulary in all classrooms*. 3rd ed. Upper Saddle River, NJ: Pearson/Merrill/Prentice Hall.

References Cited *(cont.)*

Blachowicz, C., P. Fisher, D. Ogle, and S. Watts-Taffe. 2006. Vocabulary: Questions from the classroom. *Reading Research Quarterly* 41:524–538.

Brook, D. 1998. *The journey of English.* New York: Clarion Books.

Chandler, R. E., and K. Schwartz. 1961. *A new history of Spanish literature.* Baton Rouge, LA: Louisiana State University Press.

Clemens, S. (Mark Twain). Letter to George Bainton, October 15, 1888.

Cruz, G. 2007. 10 best buzzwords of 2007. *Time*, December: 70.

Cunningham, A. E. 2005. Vocabulary growth through independent reading and reading aloud to children. In *Teaching and learning vocabulary: Bringing research to practice*, ed. E. H. Hiebert and M. L. Kamil, 45–68. Mahwah, NJ: Erlbaum.

Davis, F. 1944. Fundamental factors of comprehension in reading. *Psychometrika* 9:185–97.

Graves, M. F., and J. Fitzgerald. 2006. Effective vocabulary instruction for English-language learners. In *The vocabulary-enriched classroom*, ed. C. C. Block and J. N. Mangieri, 118–37. New York: Scholastic.

Graves, M. F., and S. M. Watts-Taffe. 2002. The place of word consciousness in a research-based vocabulary program. In *What research has to say about reading instruction*, ed. A. Farstrup and S. J. Samuels, 140–65. Newark, DE: International Reading Association.

Harmon, J. M., W. B. Hedrick, and K. D. Wood. 2005. Research on vocabulary instruction in the content areas: Implications for struggling readers. *Reading & Writing Quarterly* 21:261–80.

References Cited (cont.)

Harris, T., and R. Hodges. 1995. *The literacy dictionary.* Newark, DE: International Reading Association.

Hart, B., and T. R. Risley. 1995. *Meaningful differences in everyday experiences of young children.* Baltimore: Brookes.

——. 2003. The early catastrophe. *American Educator* (Spring): 4–9.

Haynes, J. 2007. *Getting started with English language learners.* Alexandria, VA: Association for Supervision and Curriculum Development.

Hoyt, L. 1999. *Revisit, reflect, retell: Strategies for improving reading comprehension.* Portsmouth, NH: Heinemann.

Kamil, M., and E. Hiebert. 2005. *Teaching and learning vocabulary: Bringing research to practice.* Mahwah, NJ: Erlbaum.

Lakoff, G., and M. Johnson. 1980. *Metaphors we live by.* Chicago: University of Chicago Press.

Lehr, F., J. Osborn, and E. Hiebert. *A focus on vocabulary.* Pacific Resources for Education and Learning. Accessed September 27, 2007, from http://www.prel.org/products/re_/ES0419.htm

Martin, J. 1998. *Snowflake Bentley.* Boston: Houghton Mifflin.

Marzano, R., D. Pickering, and J. Pollock. 2001. *Classroom instruction that works: Research-based strategies for increasing student achievement.* Alexandria, VA: Association for Supervision and Curriculum Development.

McCrum, R., W. Cran, and R. MacNeil. 1987. *The story of English.* New York: Penguin Books.

Merriam-Webster's Collegiate Dictionary. 11th ed. 2003. Springfield, MA: Merriam-Webster, Inc.

References Cited (cont.)

Merriam-Webster's Online Dictionary. http://www.merriam-webster.com (accessed March, 2008).

Nagy, W. 1988. *Teaching vocabulary to improve reading comprehension.* Urbana, IL: National Council of Teachers of English.

Nagy, W., and R. Anderson. 1984. How many words are there in printed school English? *Reading Research Quarterly* 19:303–30.

Nagy, W., and J. Scott. 2000. Vocabulary processes. In Vol. 3 of *Handbook of reading research*, ed. M. Kamil, P. Mosenthal, P. D. Pearson, and R. Barr, 269–84. Mahwah, NJ: Erlbaum.

Nation, I. 2001. *Learning vocabulary in another language.* Cambridge, UK: Cambridge University Press.

National Reading Panel. 2000. *Report of the National Reading Panel: Teaching children to read. Report of the subgroups.* Washington, DC: U.S. Department of Health and Human Services, National Institutes of Health.

Newton, R. M., and E. Newton. 2005. A little Latin…and a lot of English. *Adolescent Literacy in Perspective* (May). *Ohio Resource Center for Mathematics, Science, and Reading.* Retrieved January 19, 2006 from http://www.ohiorc.org/adlit/ip_content.aspx?recID=159&parentID=158

Newton, E., N. Padak, and T. Rasinski. 2008. *Evidence-based instruction in reading: A professional development guide to vocabulary instruction.* Boston: Pearson/Allyn & Bacon.

Online Etymology Dictionary. http://www.etymonline.com (accessed March, 2008).

Parish, P. 1995. *Amelia Bedelia's treasury.* New York: Harper Collins.

References Cited *(cont.)*

Pearson, P. D., E. Hiebert, and M. Kamil. 2007. Vocabulary assessment: What we know and what we need to learn. *Reading Research Quarterly* 42:282–96.

Perez, B. 2004. Language, literacy, and biliteracy. In *Sociocultural contexts of language and literacy*. 2nd ed. Ed. B. Perez, 25–56. Mahwah, NJ: Erlbaum.

Random House Webster's College Dictionary. 2005. New York: Random House Reference.

Rasinski, T. 2001. *Making and writing words (grades 3–6).* Greensboro, NC: Carson-Dellosa Publishing.

Rasinski, T., and N. Padak. 2001. *From phonics to fluency.* New York: Longman.

———. 2004. *Effective reading strategies.* 3rd ed. Upper Saddle River, NJ: Pearson/Merrill Prentice Hall.

Rasinski, T., N. Padak, R. Newton, and E. Newton. 2006. *Building vocabulary from word roots (levels 3–8).* Huntington Beach, CA: Teacher Created Materials (Beach City Press).

Romans, The. (n.d.) London: The Watts Publishing Company. Retrieved December 17, 2007, from http://www.orchardbooks.co.uk/fwmain1.htm

Roosevelt, F. D. 1941. Quote accessed at http://www.archives.gov/education/lessons/day-of-infamy

Schotter, R. 2006. *The boy who loved words.* New York: Schwartz Wade Books.

Shulman, M. 2006. *Mom and dad are palindromes.* San Francisco: Chronicle Books.

Silverstein, S. 2005. *Where the sidewalk ends.* New York: Scholastic, Inc.

References Cited (cont.)

Stahl, S. 1986. Three principles of effective vocabulary instruction. *Journal of Reading* 29:662–71.

———. 1992. Saying the "p" word: Nine guidelines for exemplary phonics instruction. *The Reading Teacher* 45:618–25.

Stahl, S., and M. Fairbanks. 1986. The effects of vocabulary instruction: A model-based meta-analysis. *Review of Educational Research* 56:72–110.

Sweet, A. P., and C. E. Snow, eds. 2003. *Rethinking reading comprehension*. New York: Guilford Press.

Waugh, E. 1962. Quote accessed at http://history.enotes.com/famous-quotes.

Weaver, C. 2002. *Reading process and practice*. 3rd ed. Portsmouth, NH: Heinemann.

White, T. G., J. Sowell, and A. Yanagihara. 1989. Teaching elementary students to use word-part clues. *The Reading Teacher* 42:302–9.